TRANSGENERATIONAL RESILIENCY

UNLOCK THE STRENGTH IN YOUR DNA

JOSEPH LATHAM, PSY.D.

CONTENTS

ISBN-13: 979-8-218-15282-6

There has always been a dissonance between the negative messages I heard and the beauty I saw with my eyes. This book is dedicated to those who reinforced my strengths and supported me even when I didn't know it. To my Grandparents, Mother, Sister, Aunties, Uncles, Cuzzos, and Wife—you have taught me how strong we are through your actions. To my children—focus on your self-confidence. No one can take that away from you, except yourself. Last, I would like to dedicate this to all the countless African-American stories that have reinforced my beliefs about how amazing our people truly are.

This is my culture.

INTRODUCTION

She wore a bow in her hair.

When I look at the picture of Ruby Bridges, just six years old when she integrated William J. Frantz Elementary School, the thing that jumps out to me is that crisp, white bow. Her mother must have known what she would face that day. Hordes of white people stood near the school. They hurled insults at that six-year-old with the bright, genuine smile.

But still, she dressed in her best school clothes. Little black patent leather shoes. Clean white cuffed socks. A dress with a gathered skirt. And a plaid bag.

And on top of it all, her mother added a bow to her hair. When I see that picture, I think of strength. Little Ruby

Bridges refused to buckle under pressure. Even when she knew that she was about to walk through something terrible, she showed up in her Sunday best.

After all, she was fulfilling a legacy of so many people's wills and wishes.

I wonder whether she knew what it meant. At such a young age, could she have even known how strong she was? This little girl carried the future of her people on her shoulders. Just six years old, she stood tall under a level of pressure that would bring most men to their knees. And yet she marched bravely into war, with nothing to support her but an unbreakable spirit.

But even though she didn't know it, Ruby Bridges had a lot going for her.

She was far from the first African American to walk through hell. Generations of Black men, women, and children before her had experienced the same struggle. And they were all there with her, giving her strength, resiliency, and optimism.

I don't mean that metaphorically.

In a very literal way, Ruby Bridges's DNA prepared her to do what she did that day. By November 14, 1960—the day she walked up the steps to her new school—generations of African Americans had lived and died under the same types of discrimination Bridges would help to end.

This book is about how those who came before her—those who came before us—make our brains and bodies stronger than any other group of people in the world.

Ruby Bridges didn't know it, but she had the strength of her ancestors in her DNA. And, while her famous walk happened decades ago, that lesson is more important today than ever before.

THE URGENCY OF TRANSGENERATIONAL RESILIENCY

Since the disturbing murder of George Floyd in the summer of 2020, it seems like everyone has something to say about race. Whether they're talking about diversity and inclusion, equity, racial justice, or some other term, American culture is full of people with opinions on racism. People, particularly white people, who had never given a second thought to African American rights suddenly popped out of the woodwork, ready to lead the charge.

Most of them focused on suffering.

They searched history for our most gaping wounds. They talked about massacres and exploitation. They talked about horrifying medical experiments. They talked about lynching and death.

It was hard not to see some of their faces light up as they explained our ancestors' suffering.

Those barriers were real—and some of them still are. But the reason we know so much about them is that so many of our powerful ancestors survived. That's what gets lost in current discussions of diversity, equity, and inclusion. When we focus on the suffering, we miss the strength. When we focus on the hardships, we miss the power.

When we focus on the rejections, we miss the resiliency. This book is about that resiliency. It's about a physiological,

psychological phenomenon that carried generations of African Americans through hell. Using cutting-edge research in neuroscience, behavioral psychology, and clinical mental health treatment, I introduce a trait that all African Americans have—we just don't know it yet.

I call it transgenerational resiliency.

As I'll explain throughout this book, transgenerational resiliency comes from the power of trauma to reshape who we are—through generations of challenges, our ancestors became stronger and wiser, and they've passed those traits on to us. And while the barriers African Americans have faced along the way are included in this book—they're part of our history—this book isn't about barriers.

It's about encountering the toughest, angriest, most persistent blockades and laughing in their faces. That's the kind of power that comes from transgenerational resiliency.

Focusing on the strength, power, and wisdom of our ancestors will change your life. As a clinical psychologist, I've worked with dozens of clients who have turned their lives around. Many of the people I've worked with are in prison. Others came to me with daily anxiety. Some believed they had to act "white" if they wanted to succeed.

In all of these cases, learning about transgenerational resiliency changed their entire approach. They were able to tap into the gifts of their ancestors—the gifts described in this book—and activate their unique power.

This book is for African Americans who want to understand themselves as powerful, strong, wise individuals. While I discuss many key moments in Black history, from the transatlantic slave trade to Jim Crow to segregation and beyond, I focus on the strength inside *your DNA*.

Because those events aren't just history. They exist inside you.

And this book will help you find them.

PART ONE
EPIGENETICS

CHAPTER 1
THE DSM WASN'T WRITTEN FOR US

IMAGINE yourself seated in a gray upholstered chair. Across from you, an older white man scribbles something in a small notebook. He glances up at you periodically.

"Just a minute," he says. "My last appointment ran over."

"It's okay," you reply.

The chair, you realize, is less comfortable than it looked. Your back begins to ache, and you shift your weight, but the tension rises in your shoulders and neck.

Maybe it's not the chair at all. This is, after all, your first counseling session. The office is quiet except for the hum of the air conditioner, and you're not sure what you're supposed to do while he writes.

"Okay." The man smiles—it looks forced. "Shall we begin?"

You nod as he reaches into his desk drawer and retrieves a manilla file folder. He places it on his desk and looks up at you, his face a mask of calm. "I'm going to show you a series of pictures," he says. "I want you to tell me what you see."

He slips a thick card from the folder and holds it between his hands, the base of the paper resting on the desk. Printed on the card is an image of a white child and a violin. Head propped between his hands, the boy frowns down at the instrument.

Peering over the photo at you, the man says, "Tell me a story about this image."

This scene is far from what my counseling clients experience, but, unfortunately, it's not uncommon in the history of Psychology. From the older white male psychologist to the picture of the little boy, the scene encapsulates much about the field's traditions.

The picture the man holds is the first of a series—in the next image, a muscular white man climbs a rope. Then, a white woman gazes off into the distance. Finally, a white woman climbs a flight of stairs, and another glances behind her as a white man works in a field.

Together, these photos form the Thematic Apperception Test—the TAT. Like the more commonly recognized Rorschach test, the TAT is a projective test. In all projective tests, a person is shown an ambiguous image and asked to describe what they see. Their answer reveals something about their personality.

We project ourselves onto the image, the theory goes; so when we describe the image, we actually describe ourselves.

When the psychologist shows you the picture of the boy with the violin, he hopes to uncover your feelings about childhood. Psychologists chose the young white boy to represent a universal child, and the boy's disappointed expression to represent failure. According to the test's developers, the image should remind us of difficult times in our childhood. We project those feeling onto the boy, describe them to our counselor, and work together to process those buried feelings.

This diagnostic tool assumes that everyone can identify with the child in the picture. We are supposed to see ourselves in the boy, and, in describing him, we describe ourselves.

But I don't see myself in the boy.

When I look at this image, I have more questions than answers.

I wonder why the child has a violin. I wonder what it might feel like to hold a violin, and whether this young child can play the instrument. I wonder whether there is something about playing the violin that made him sad or angry. And, frankly, I feel a little annoyed at the kid. If his biggest concern in this world is that violin, I don't have much sympathy for him.

As an African American man who has never owned a violin, I find the image unrelatable. I don't recognize myself in that sad white boy. No matter how I describe him, I'm always describing *him*. I'm never describing *myself*.

The researchers and subjects who first tested the TAT probably related to the white boy with the violin, because the test targeted a very specific cultural group. Originally designed and tested in the 1930s, the subjects were all students at Harvard, Yale, and Radcliffe. The average age was twenty-two years old.

And every single one of them was white.

Based on the demographics of the people in their experience, the TAT's creators knew nothing about people of other races, ages, or socioeconomic statuses. They just knew that wealthy white twenty-two-year-olds related to the boy. And because those subjects related to the boy, the researchers assumed that *everyone* could relate to the boy.

Later researchers explicitly cautioned psychologists from using the test for people beyond the original demographic. And yet, the TAT has been used for decades to make all sorts of harmful claims. Sometimes these claims are subtle. A person who thinks the boy is lucky might be diagnosed as a narcissist—many white psychologists believe that a failure to identify the boy's sadness reflects a person's inability to identify their own weaknesses. Someone who simply says the boy is sad might be diagnosed with depression, with the psychologist reasoning that their own bad feelings about childhood were too painful to discuss.

Other times, the diagnoses are much more sinister. White psychologists have used the TAT to argue that Black people are more likely to be violent, that Latino people are more likely to be lazy, and that Asian people are more likely to be submissive.

All based on the assumption that everyone can relate to a little white boy with a violin.

I can't relate to him. I suspect you can't either.

That doesn't mean we are "less than." It doesn't mean we are defective or depressed or narcissistic. It just means we have nothing in common with the little white boy with the violin.

And it means the TAT was not made for us.

Unfortunately, the TAT is far from the only psychological test with racist implications. The majority of psychological diagnoses and treatments were developed for white patients by white psychologists.

Throughout this book, I'll present alternative Interpretations of psychology's taken-for-granted assumptions about African Americans. Most of these assumptions come from white patients and researchers who see their experiences as universal. Just as the TAT assumes that all patients can see themselves in a little boy with a violin, the field of psychology has always used white experiences as the standard.

This book isn't about white people. It's about helping African Americans find more useful applications of psychology, despite the field's white history. So, before we activate our Transgenerational Resiliency, let's sift through Psychology to determine which parts are helpful, and which are harmful.

To do that, we need to talk about White Psychology.

WHITE PSYCHOLOGY AND THE RACISM OF STANDARDIZATION

For generations, white researchers studied people who looked like them, who came from the same cultural, educational, and economic backgrounds. Then they took the results and declared them universal. The ideas were never tested on African Americans. They don't consider African American needs or experiences. But they are applied to African Americans just the same.

This is White Psychology.

Take, for example, the Stanford-Binet Intelligence Test. More commonly known as the IQ test, this test was first developed in the early 1900s by white French psychologist Alfred Binet. Binet saw intelligence as a combination of genetics and environment, or nature and nurture. With the goal to create a standardized scale, he developed a series of cognitive tasks that became the gold standard for intelligence measurement. The tasks ranged from simple, like naming objects, to more complex, like solving math problems.

The test is one of the most commonly used IQ tests in the world. Used by schools, businesses, and organizations to measure intelligence, Binet's test has elevated countless people to genius status—and declared just as many stupid.

IQ testing poses a number of problems. Unreliable at best, the test results vary depending on when and how the tests are administered. IQ tests claim to offer objective results, but they rely on the subjective opinions of the administrator who interprets them. And they can only measure the types of intelligence Binet saw as important.

But the biggest problem with the Stanford-Binet test is its racism.

In the early 1900s, psychologists Henry Goddard and Lewis Terman brought the Stanford-Binet Test to America. The test, they argued, was an objective measure of intelligence that could be used to determine which children belonged in schools. Using scores interpreted by white psychologists—and ignoring the fact that Black children had little or no access to Math and Reading—Goddard and Terman suggested that African American children's test scores indicated a lack of intelligence. In a time of heated public education debates, their argument helped to deny Black children an education.

Standardized tests remain a staple in formulas for public school funding, college admissions, job placements, and psychological diagnoses. Often, African Americans score lower on these tests, just as they did in the 1900s.

But the problem is not African American children. The problem is standardization.

Every person on this planet has strengths and weaknesses. Some of us whiz through complicated algebra equations. Some effortlessly adapt to others' moods. Some of us can visualize every move on a chess board. Others make beautiful clothing or remember their family members' birthdays or hit a baseball into the gap in the outfield.

All of these are important skills. But only one is routinely measured through standardized tests.

Think about your biggest strength—the thing you do best. If someone designed a test around that particular skill, you'd ace it. You probably wouldn't feel nervous to take that test. In fact, you'd probably feel pretty great when you finished. On a scale of one to one hundred, you'd probably score somewhere in the 80s or 90s. Let's imagine you score a 97.

Now imagine if someone designed a test around your biggest weakness. The thought is daunting. You'd perform significantly worse at that test. In fact, you might even try to skip the test altogether. You might feel physically sick as you awaited the start of the exam. You might be tempted to give up. That score will look a lot different—let's say a 62.

If someone compared the first score—a 97, with the second—a 62, they'd most likely imagine two very different people. The person who scored a 97 is exceptional! The person who scored a 62 struggles to keep up.

But they aren't two different people. They're both you.

Whether you're taking the test that emphasizes your strengths or the one that emphasizes your weaknesses, you're the same person. You're valuable. You have things to offer the world. You care for others, and others care for you.

You are the same person.

But your scores will be very different.

Now imagine everyone in your city had to take one of those tests, and the results determined where they were allowed to live, whether they could attend school, how much money they earned, and who their kids could play with.

Is the test fairer or more objective if it measures your strengths?

Of course not!

You deserve the same housing options, the same schools, the same career access, and family stability regardless of your score on a test. While the test may be objective, in that everyone receives the same test form and the same instructions, someone had to decide what the test should include.

If those choices are arbitrary, the test isn't objective at all.

Yet, White Psychology has built an empire on the assumption that tests can be objective and, therefore, standardized.

This is the racism of standardization, at least as it is practiced in American Psychology. White psychologists design a test, often with the goal of measuring something the researcher has observed in their own community. That test is administered to others in their cultural group, and the results are collected, analyzed, and published.

Under the assumption that the test is objective, psychological researchers around the country administer the test to different cultural groups—people with different strengths than the white researcher's cultural group. But rather than determining that the test is subjective, researchers declare the other cultural group inferior. The process is repeated again and again until it becomes a staple of the field—a standardized test.

Standardization is the backbone of White Psychology. White researchers design tests to measure white strengths. By administering the test to hundreds of white test subjects, the researchers determine an average score. The test is then administered to African Americans. And when our scores fall outside the average, *we* are found lacking. Never the tests.

A single reference book distills the results of generations of flawed tests. Used to diagnose and treat people from all cultures, backgrounds, and experiences, this book claims objectivity despite its foundation in White Psychology. This book, displayed in counseling offices across the country, is called the DSM.

STANDARDIZING TRAUMA

The DSM, or Diagnostic and Statistical Manual of Mental Disorders, is the definitive reference book for all psychological conditions. Comprised of generations of studies, it is a resource so trusted that its results are often taken for granted.

But the foundation of the book is White Psychology. It wasn't written for us.

I'm not alone in my criticisms of the DSM. Many experts—chiefly African American psychologists like me—argue that the DSM perpetuates racism by measuring all patients against a white middle-class standard. This means that African Americans are often inaccurately diagnosed with some mental disorders while others go unrecognized.

The DSM might tell someone they're a narcissist because they can't relate to a sad white boy with a violin.

The DSM might tell someone they're stupid because they scored a 62 on a standardized test.

And the DSM might diagnose all African Americans with trauma.

Or, more specifically, *white psychologists* might use the DSM to diagnose all African Americans with trauma.

I've often found myself in rooms full of white psychologists as they use the DSM to understand particular patterns of thought. Running the theoretical gamut, the group will raise issues from personality disorders to emotional regulation to developmental psychology, all described in detail in the DSM.

As soon as the subject of Black mental health arises, the conversation turns to trauma.

"There's a lot to work through," one white woman will say. "African Americans' fear of dogs, for example. It's because of the trauma they experienced during the Civil Rights movement."

The frustration starts to rise in my chest.

"Yes, and that's the reason so many of them can't swim," a young white man adds. He glances over at me, the only African American in the room. "I mean, people of color," he clarifies.

No matter how many times I hear it, I can never believe what I'm hearing.

"The fear gets passed on. Through generations." "They can't help it."

Finally, I interject. "What Black people are you talking about?" I ask.

A flush rises in the woman's chest, but the man presses on, "Transgenerational trauma."

Transgenerational trauma. It's been a buzzword in psychology circles for at least a decade. I don't begrudge people who find the term useful for understanding their own difficulties. But I do have a problem with the way White Psychology uses the term to replace all other theories of Black mental health.

Whether or not people discuss trauma in a compassionate way, the result is the same—trauma becomes the focus, never strength, resiliency, joy, or endurance.

"What you're saying doesn't describe *me* or anyone I know," I press on. "It's false. Why are we teaching this to our students?"

The comment always stuns the room. It's as though many of these white psychologists haven't considered the full range of African American experiences—and I suspect they haven't.

I get legitimately angry every time this scene plays out.

Because you could put an inner-city African American kid next to a middle-class white kid and ask them both to write a paper. The inner-city kid might struggle, but he'll find a way through. His life hasn't been easy—the challenge of writing a paper is nothing to him.

The middle-class white kid, on the other hand, usually has much less mental toughness. He hasn't needed to be strong. He doesn't know how. Maybe he knows how to write the paper. But if he doesn't, he'll crumble.

I'll bet on the Black kid every time. His experiences have built a resiliency that is undoubtedly unknown to the white psychologists.

That resiliency is the ace in our pocket, and every African American reading this book has it. But we'll never activate our resiliency as long as we are focused on our trauma. The DSM identifies our trauma because White Psychology only cares about our weaknesses—it only cares about comparing us to white middle-class students at Harvard.

If it measured our resiliency, we'd score a 97 every time.

FROM WHITE PSYCHOLOGY TO AFRICAN AMERICAN RESILIENCY

White Psychology was designed to discourage African American strength and resiliency. But Black Americans have withstood its discriminatory effects. Generations of African Americans have found ways of processing difficulties and emerging on the other side with increased capacity for strength, drive, ambition, health, and success.

With our unique capacity for resiliency in the face of trauma, we can achieve anything we set our minds to. But first, we have to tap into our history and embrace the strength of our ancestors.

It's not about Transgenerational Trauma. It's about Transgenerational Resiliency.

In the next chapter, I'll explore the powerful gift of African American history. Generations of Black Americans have proven that challenges only make us stronger, even if these strengths aren't valued by standardized testing. These are history's multiplication tables, and they're embedded in your DNA.

CHAPTER 2
HISTORY'S MULTIPLICATION TABLES

THREE PICTURES HANG on my living room wall. In the first, my great-grandfather stares forward, jaw set and eyes confident below the brim of a uniform cap. My grandfather grins in the second. Dressed in his army uniform, he looks directly into the camera. The third is a picture of me in my own military uniform. Like a timeline, the two men pictured to my left predict my life's journey.

I got a lot from those men. Not just the shape of my eyes, which aren't so different from my grandfather's. And not only my smile—a toothy grin I inherited from my grandfather. Those men also gave me strength, resiliency, tenacity, and determination; traits that carried me through my military career and into the field of Psychology.

Whether displayed on the wall or in a photo album, most of us have similar pictures that document the stories of our lives. They tell us why our face is round or why our ears stick out. When we talk about these physical features, we're talking about genetics.

But our genes contain lots of hidden information, too. If your father's eyelashes are short and your mother's are long, you'll inherit both genes. You might not need false lashes, but your DNA still contains the short-eyelash gene, hidden within your DNA's *code*. When you apply mascara in the morning, you're looking at your genetic *expression*: the effects of that code. The difference between code and expression is the reason lifestyle changes can prevent disease—even if your DNA contains the code for cancer, particular experiences can discourage that code from expressing itself.

Epigenetics is the study of how our DNA expression changes. Most of us think of DNA as something that happens from the inside out. From the time we're born, our genes tell our bodies what to look like, how to behave—even which foods we like. But epigenetics tells us that we can also change our DNA from the *outside in*. Particular behaviors and experiences encode themselves on our DNA, changing our traits by changing our genetic expression.

Imagine a boxer. Every day, he works his muscles to the point of exhaustion. Every night, he's asleep the second his head hits the pillow. He takes a lot of hits when he fights, but he never quits. Boxing isn't just his livelihood—it's also his passion.

There are probably aspects of his DNA that predispose him to boxing. Tall and lanky, he got his height from his mother's side and his quick, thin physique from his father's. But there's much more to championship boxing than a tall, slim physique. Boxing also takes long hours of training. After hours at the gym, boxers must stick to a strict diet. And all of that culminates in taking hit after hit in the ring.

Boxing takes a lot of determination and grit.

Over the years, the stress of training may change the way a boxer's DNA expresses itself. Those hours in the gym, that strict diet, and the uppercuts to the jaw don't just change his body—they also change the way he responds to stress, pain, and fatigue. Early in his career, his DNA may have told him to flee at the first sign of danger. By his third prize fight, he's repressed that urge. He'll retire having altered the expression of his DNA through sheer force of will.

He wasn't born boxing, but his children may inherit the toughness and determination he worked years to build.

That's epigenetics.

When people talk about Transgenerational Trauma, they're referring to epigenetics. The concept of Transgenerational Trauma refers to the way extreme stress epigenetically encodes itself onto our DNA, changing its expression. That shift in coding can be passed on to future generations. In the case of Transgenerational Trauma, we might view this as a burden—the children and grandchildren of people who experienced trauma have the weight of suffering in their DNA.

For African Americans, this means the struggle of being kidnapped from our home continent is encoded on our DNA. Generations of enslavement followed by generations of white violence are encoded on our DNA. The segregation, discrimination, and abuse of our parents and grandparents are encoded on our DNA.

Those experiences were traumatic.

But when I look at them, I don't see a history of trauma. I see a history of strength. I see a gift of resiliency that your great-great-grandparents gave you, even though you never met them. You might not realize it's there—it's hidden in your DNA—but it's inside you. And with each new generation of struggle, it has doubled in size, making you unstoppable.

HOW RESILIENCY DOUBLES WITH EACH GENERATION

What does it mean to be unstoppable? What does it mean to be resilient? Some definitions compare resiliency to a rubber band. When stretched and released, a strong rubber band springs back to its original size. Stretching the band puts stress on it, but it is resilient—it maintains its shape and size through the stress. While the stretch might mark the band at a microscopic level, a strong rubber band can withstand the stress and bounce back without a second thought.

That's resiliency—the ability to bounce back from stressful situations. In this standard definition, everyone has resiliency. We can all survive some level of stress. Our own capacity for resiliency is individual, dependent on a variety of factors ranging from environment to personality.

But epigenetics tells us that stress—the stretching of that band, microscopic damage included—can be passed from generation to generation.

So can resiliency.

Transgenerational Resiliency is the armor of history. It's a type of strength—an ability to bounce back—that our ancestors gave us before we were even born. To really understand how Transgenerational Resiliency works, let's look back at history's multiplication tables.

1839, Sierra Leone

In 1839, captors visited what is now Sierra Leone and abducted a little girl named Kag'ne. She was forced onto a Spanish ship with five hundred men, women, and children from at least nine different tribes. Subjected to unthinkable conditions, many of the kidnapped died. Others, including Kag'ne, made it, barely alive, to the Cuban coast. There, she was sold to a Spanish slave owner, along with fifty-three other people, several of them children like her. The enslaved people were loaded onto a ship—the Amistad—to be transported to a sugar plantation. Adults on the ship knew their odds of returning home were shrinking by the day. So in the early morning hours of July 2, the kidnapped passengers broke free from their shackles. Led by a man named Sengbe Pieh, they revolted against the ship's crew, murdering several of their captors. They forced two experienced crewmembers to steer the ship back to West Africa.

They didn't make it home—at least not yet. The navigators took the ship north where it docked at Long Island. Despite the horrific experiences they had endured, the passengers found themselves at the center of a legal battle. The surviving Africans, including Kag'ne, would wait years for the US to recognize their freedom.

In the end, abolitionists raised funds to sail them back to their homes, and the thirty-five survivors were returned to Africa. Many reunited with family. Others—including Kag'ne—remained with American missionaries.

Kag'ne's story is exceptional in that the rebellion successfully returned many kidnapped Africans to their rightful homes. But the enslavement of children was not unusual at all. In the North Atlantic slave trade, children were seen as particularly valuable, their minds more pliable and their bodies weaker.

It's horrifying to imagine what they must have gone through—what they must have seen. Exposed to kidnapping, unspeakable conditions, death, and murder, Kag'ne saw more suffering before the age of ten than most people experience throughout their lives.

Other enslaved children lived out their lives on plantations, growing into adults who never experienced freedom.

But they survived.

They are our ancestors. Their DNA survives through their descendants.

1920, Paris, Texas

Eighty years later, Millie Arthur was just fourteen when her brothers were murdered. Her family sharecropped on a white family's farm in Texas. Sharecropping arrangements were heavily skewed in favor of the farm owners—this often trapped African Americans in lives akin to their enslaved ancestors. So, while the Arthur boys were supposed to have time off on Saturdays and Sundays, the farm's owners John and Will Hodges routinely pressured them to work longer hours.

Sometime in the summer of 1920, the Hodges went to the Arthur home to torment the family. They tossed their dinner from the stove to the ground. They threw out their furniture. And they made Millie and her two sisters strip off their dresses.

When the family tried to flee a few days later, the Hodges appeared and shot at the family. One of the Arthur boys ran inside the house, retrieved a shotgun, and killed Will and John Hodges.

Fleeing for their lives, the family made it as far as Oklahoma before they were retrieved and brought back to Texas. Millie and her sisters were taken into custody where they were beaten, raped, and held captive in the basement. Millie's brothers Herman and Ervie were lynched, their bodies paraded through the town's African American neighborhoods.

Millie witnessed harassment and murder. She was sexually assaulted. She was beaten bloody. She experienced the horror of running, only to be caught and dragged back to hell.

But she survived. So many Black teenage girls experienced these horrors in the early twentieth century and went on to have families of their own.

They are our ancestors.

1991, Los Angeles, California

Sixty-one years later, fourteen-year-old Shinese lost her cousin. Shinese and Latasha had been inseparable. Born just a year apart, they came of age together in Los Angeles. Latasha's mother had been murdered in an LA nightclub just six years earlier, when the girl was only nine, and Latasha and Shinese clung to each other for strength.

One evening, Latasha stopped by a neighborhood convenience store. With two dollars in her hand, she picked up a $1.79 bottle of orange juice. The shop owner grabbed Latasha, accusing her of stealing. The young girl fled for the door, but she didn't make it. The shop owner, Soon Ja Du, fired a single shot into the back of her head, killing her instantly.

Shinese was left to pick up the pieces after losing her cousin—her best friend. Around her, the city burned as people from around the country reacted to Rodney King's brutal beating at the hands of LAPD.

Barely a teenager, Shinese survived the tragedy, going on to tell her cousin's story.

Like Kag'ne and Millie before her, Shinese survived in the face of incredible suffering.

Today

Against all odds, African Americans have survived generations of violence. We survived kidnapping and enslavement. Through the violence of Jim Crow, we survived. We fought back through the Civil Rights era, our brothers and sisters falling all around us. And we survived that, too.

These experiences are inside of us. But they don't just show us our ancestors' pain.

They show us their strength.

It takes a lot to endure this kind of targeted, multi-generational violence. Many of our ancestors didn't make it. But those who survived became stronger—all the way down to their DNA.

Transgenerational Resiliency isn't just about one individual. Transgenerational Resiliency is about the cumulative effects of struggle.

Let's go all the way back to Kag'ne, experiencing the unthinkable aboard the Amistad in 1839. By the very definition of the word, she was resilient—the stress she endured must have stretched that rubber band to its limits. She lived through hell and came out a survivor. That kind of stress alters a person, encoding not just her trauma—but her resiliency—onto her DNA.

We don't know much about what happened to Kag'ne after the Supreme Court declared her freedom. But we do know that many girls like her grew up to raise families in America. Born with an extra layer of resiliency, Kag'ne's children received a gift that was stronger than their mother's captors.

The torment of African Americans certainly didn't stop with Kag'ne. Her children lived through the fires of the Civil War and the hope of Reconstruction. And when Reconstruction was toppled by a racist government, they saw the violence of Jim Crow.

Kag'ne's resiliency was in their DNA. And they added resiliency of their own, doubling their own children's genetic toughness.

Of course, it wasn't just the mothers who suffered—the fathers did, too. And for each mother and father who survived the hell fires of American racism, a child was born with twice the genetic strength of their parents—twice the capacity for their DNA to express itself as resiliency, strength, and grit.

So by the time Millie Arthur was born in 1907, five generations of African American ancestors had built her up. What began as Kag'ne's thin layer of epigenetic protection doubled over on itself five times.

And what began as Millie's thick epigenetic protection continued to double through the Civil Rights era with its church bombings, fire-hoses, dogs, and assassinations.

By the time Shinese was born in the late 1970s, African Americans had built up generations of epigenetic resiliency. Our DNA had been changed, encoded with the strength our ancestors brought due to the terror they lived through. It no doubt helped Shinese to survive the horrific murder of her cousin—and to find a platform to tell Latasha's story.

Encoded with the power to survive, we all have that strength inside us—it's the ultimate gift of our ancestors.

POST-TRAUMATIC GROWTH

When we're confronted with history's horror stories, it can be challenging to focus on strength and resiliency. But throughout this book, I'll encourage you to do just that. One tool that can help is the concept of Post-Traumatic Growth.

In the previous chapter, I argued that the DSM—Psychology's reference book for diagnosis and treatment—wasn't written with African Americans in mind. This is never clearer than when we look back at our ancestors' suffering.

The most recent edition of the DSM defines trauma as: Exposure to actual or threatened death, serious injury, or sexual violence in one (or more) of the following ways: directly experiencing the traumatic event(s); witnessing, in person, the traumatic event(s) as it occurred to others; learning that the traumatic event(s) occurred to a close family member or close friend...or experiencing repeated or extreme exposure to aversive details of the traumatic event(s).[1] Kag'ne checked every single one of those boxes: death, serious injury, and sexual violence; both directly and as a witness to others. Millie, too. So did your ancestors. Even if you haven't directly experienced these traumatic events, I'll bet you've seen videos of African American men and women killed for no reason but the color of their skin—the color of *our* skin.

The effects of these experiences—whether direct or through witness—can include upsetting, unwanted thoughts. Many people avoid thinking about the violence they've seen or experienced. We might feel isolated or angry, or notice changes in our moods.

These effects—unwanted thoughts, avoidance, anger—are the DSM's requirements for Post-Traumatic Stress Disorder. And most African Americans have experienced them at least once.

So how do we survive? How do we keep on going about our day? How do we drive or go jogging or have children when we live with constant reminders of the pain of recent and past history?

The answer is Post-Traumatic Growth.

African Americans have been gifted by our ancestors with Transgenerational Resiliency. Like a superpower, the strength locked into our DNA allows us to move beyond experiences that could be debilitating for others. We never fight our battles on our own—we always have generations of Black men and women in our corner.

In this way, trauma is not a crushing, defeating syndrome.

It's the very thing that makes us stronger.

Of course, I'm not urging African Americans—or anybody—to seek out trauma. Trauma is harmful. Our ancestors undoubtedly wished they could avoid it. They didn't look for trauma. It came for them.

But they didn't crumble in the face of trauma either. Most African Americans have a particular ability to walk through suffering and come out stronger on the other side. Our ancestors stood firm and proud as the world collapsed around them. They turned history's horrors into a gift.

That's Post-Traumatic Growth.

Post-Traumatic Growth means transforming our struggles into strength. It means focusing on what we *can* do—the power we *do* have—rather than the things that bring us down. Shifting our mindset to the positive isn't easy, but it is simple. Particularly when generations of ancestors have your back.

Resiliency is in our DNA. But that doesn't mean our lives are easy. Every day we face a new set of obstacles—discrimination, racial aggression, and violence. We approach these with the strength of our ancestors.

In the next chapter, we'll harness the power of our brains to fully tap into our ancestors' strength. But first, let's take a moment to reflect on the gifts they've given us.

EXERCISE: LEGACIES OF STRUGGLE

This exercise asks you to reflect on the Transgenerational Resiliency that's buried in your DNA. Everyone can do this, whether you knew your parents, grandparents, or great-grandparents, or whether you can only imagine them.

As with all exercises in this book, complete them on your own time, in your own way. I suggest you talk through your answers with a trusted friend or family member, but you may choose to write them down instead. You might even want to do both, writing your answers, then talking them through with someone else. If you have living relatives, this may also be an opportunity to reach out to them and ask about your family's particular challenges.

However you approach the exercise, remember to open your mind and avoid self-judgment. The point is simply to reflect on all the strength that's buried in your DNA.

Reflect on the following questions, one at a time.

Parents

Think about your parents. Picture them as younger people, perhaps your own age.

What were they like?

What kinds of things did they want in life?

What barriers did they face as they tried to achieve their goals? Consider societal, economic, academic, or environmental challenges that your parents endured.

Grandparents

Now think about your grandparents.

When they were younger, before your parents were born, what kinds of goals did they have? If you're not sure, ask a family member or make your best guess.

What kinds of societal, economic, academic, or environmental challenges did they face?

How did they respond?

Great-grandparents

Imagine your great-grandparents. If you met them when you were a young child—or not at all—just use your imagination. But try to think of them as they were when they were your current age. What was their life like?

What were some of the societal, economic, academic, or environmental challenges they faced as young adults?

How did they survive those difficulties?

Ancestors

Finally, let your mind wander back generations, to early African Americans. You've probably read about their lives or seen reenactments in movies and television shows. Try to think about a specific early African American—someone who was your ancestor.

What societal, economic, academic, or environmental challenges did they face?

How did they survive?

What were their biggest hopes?

Lineage

Imagining this lineage—from early African Americans to your great-grandparents to your grandparents to your parents—were your ancestors successful? Why or why not?

Reflection

Once you've answered these questions, take some time to reflect on what you said or wrote. Revisit this exercise if you think of other ideas or if you learn more about your lineage.

As you reflect on your ancestors' success, consider this: What if their only job was to keep their legacy alive?

How does that change your understanding of their challenges?

CHAPTER 3
THE RESTRUCTURING BRAIN

KEN GRIFFEY, Jr. was three years old when his dad played his first major league game. Ken Griffey, Sr. was a strong player, sporting three all-star games and two World Series wins. Together, the two became the first father-son duo to take to the professional baseball field at the same time. But as strong as Griffey Sr.'s record was, his son surpassed him, racking up ten Golden Glove awards and nabbing a spot in baseball's Hall of Fame.

Was Griffey, Jr.'s talent genetic? Or did he simply learn from watching his dad?

Probably a little of both.

Psychology tells us that our brains are a mixture of inherited and developed traits—often called nature and nurture.

The former—nature—includes the things we're born with. A child born to two rocket scientists might show natural talent in a classroom or lab. Another, whose parents are extroverted, might make friends easily. Depending on genetics, kids might show an innate interest in numbers, a natural talent in the kitchen, or an ability to sense others' emotions. Scientists vary in their opinions about inherited personality traits, but epigenetics tells us that we inherit some of our strengths and weaknesses from our parents.

But many of our skills and talents—as well as our shortcomings—are the result of learned behavior, or nurture. Maybe you grew up watching your grandfather garden. If so, you've probably got a better idea of which plants are dying and which are just dormant. Or, if you grew up in a musical home, you might have a strong sense of rhythm and phrasing. Simply listening to music can help kids absorb its structure and sound. And the son of a professional baseball player is likely to learn a few things about the sport, even before they're old enough for Little League.

But, with all of these examples, it's difficult to separate which aspects are genetic and which are learned. The reason is simple: nature and nurture *aren't* separate. Through epigenetics and myelination—two concepts I'll discuss in this chapter—nature and nurture work together. Nature gives us a natural ability to adapt, and nurture shapes that adaptation. Imagine a young Ken Griffey Jr., playing catch with his dad. Like all children, his first tries were probably pretty rough, landing several feet short of their target. Some of them probably strayed far to the left of his waiting father. Landing a toss in his dad's glove, at least at first, would have been a celebration—something that didn't happen often.

But as he grew—and as he and his dad played more—he improved. His arms got stronger. His aim grew surer. If he focused, he could land every toss in his dad's glove. And soon, he didn't even have to focus. Playing catch became second nature. He and his dad could talk while they played, or he could let his mind wander. The pathway from Jr.'s hand to Sr.'s glove was clear and practiced. He never missed.

No one is *born* playing catch. We all have to develop the gross motor skills to pick up and toss a ball, followed by the fine motor skills required to aim and execute a perfect throw. Griffey, Jr. learned those skills through trial and error—as we all do—along with some coaching from his dad.

But most of us would agree that the son of a professional baseball player is probably more likely to excel at sports than the rest of us.

Both men had athletic body types, stocky but slim. Both men tended toward muscular lower bodies, less useful for playing catch than for slamming six-hundred home runs out of the park. And both men demonstrated tenacity and mental strength—the resiliency of their ancestors.

This isn't nature versus nurture. It's nature and nurture combined.

But a boy learning to play catch with his all-star dad isn't just a demonstration of nature and nurture. It's also a powerful metaphor for understanding brain science.

THE SCIENCE OF MYELINATION

When someone asks your name, it probably doesn't take you long to answer—the information appears in your mind automatically. But if I asked you to name the capital of Vermont, you'd have to think about it. Even those who are well-versed in the state capitals need to search their brain to locate the information.

Why does our brain react so differently to these two requests for information? The reason may seem obvious. Your brain's ability to access your name is a product of years of practice. It's Ken Griffey, Jr. in the prime of his career, tossing a baseball across the yard to his father. Your brain's ability to access the state capital of Vermont is more like baby's first game of catch. A lot of build-up goes into gripping the ball, urging the shoulder and arm to move, and releasing at just the right time.

Saying your name feels very different from naming a state capital. But, in terms of the brain's function, they aren't so different. Every thought we have involves neural connections, or the electric impulses that fire within our brains to connect one piece of stored data with others. Questions and answers, implicit associations, political opinions, and even our feelings about friends and family all require the brain to fire in similar ways.

Imagine these neural connections as a game of catch. When

someone asks your name, the ball flies from son's hand to father's glove with ease. Naming a state capital takes more effort, but the goal is still to move the ball—the electric impulse—from point A to point B. The process is the same, but practicing makes it easier.

When we study for an exam, we're like a father teaching a son to play catch. We know the kid's throw is going to be pretty weak at first. His aim might be off. He might have trouble releasing at the right time to keep the ball in the air. So we review the information. *Smack*, the ball hits the glove. We make notecards. *Smack*. We have a friend quiz us. *Smack*. We re-read the information again. *Smack*. And with each new pass, that throw gets stronger and surer, the smack into our glove a little firmer.

Studying strengthens the neural connections in our brains. It helps train particular neurons to fire more quickly. Take an exam without studying, and you're likely to find yourself searching your brain, putting in a massive amount of effort to retrieve every bit of information. If we prepare, the information becomes much easier to retrieve.

But studying for an exam doesn't lock the information in our brains forever. Even if we know the information cold—Ken Griffey, Jr. style—if we don't revisit it for a few months, most of it will vanish without a trace. We might not be back where we started, a three-year-old struggling to grip a ball, but we won't be in all-star shape either. The information we use every day stays in tip-top shape because our brains prioritize it. But the brain's energy is limited. So as we strengthen one bit of information—one hand-to-glove connection—others atrophy.

Our brains are very good at protecting the most important pieces of information. Beyond just learning our names, our brains have to protect the neurons that fire when we raise a fork to our mouths. They have to protect the neurons that remind us not to touch a hot stove and those that flood us with love when we see our family. These are evolutionary imperatives. These neurons fire a lot—and they have to, in order to keep us safe—so our brains add an extra layer of protection around them.

This protection is called a myelin sheath. When particular neural connections fire frequently enough, this sheath wraps around the channel between the neurons. Ken Griffey, Jr. doesn't have to practice tossing a baseball every day. Through years of focus, his skills on the ball field are protected. He can hit another player's glove automatically, as though the ball was guided to the glove by an invisible track.

That track represents the myelin sheath.

Myelination—the process of producing that sheath—helps our brains develop clear, predictable pathways for moving the most important information from point A to point B. And myelination is the result of frequent, repetitive use. In some cases, the repetition is subconscious. The neural connection that tells our hearts to beat, for example, is sheathed in myelin, regardless of whether or not you ever think about your heartbeat. So is the connection that tells our lungs to expand and contract. We don't have to actively think about these processes to build up the myelin sheaths that protect them.

But just as you once learned your own name through practice and repetition, we are all capable of building intentional myelinated pathways as well. And if we repeat them enough, they become myelinated, too.

As each new day formats and reinforces that myelination, our brains are literally restructured. Reconfigured to process our most important information as quickly as possible, our brains focus on what we need every day and discard the rest. The things we practice most become natural. And this gets even easier when we practice things we were meant to practice—when we lean into the strengths of our ancestors.

GENERATIONAL MUSCLE MEMORY

When we talk about muscle memory, we're talking about our body's ability to repeat particular actions without giving them much thought. Muscle memory is what gives dancers the ability to spin effortlessly on their toes. It makes riding a bike an easy, fun activity once you get the hang of it. It's even what allows us to move our fingers quickly and thoughtlessly across a keyboard, tapping out a text message without having to search for each key. And it's what allows a major league ball player to dive for a baseball, then fling that ball across the outfield to the waiting glove of a first baseman.

We can make these actions natural by practicing them, no matter what lies in our genes. And sometimes our genetics predisposes us to these particular activities, making them even easier to conquer.

That's generational muscle memory.

Generational muscle memory is the combination of epigenetics and myelination. These two processes work together when epigenetics—the natural traits we inherit from our ancestors—combine with hard work and practice.

We've already talked about the genetic inheritance of our ancestors' strengths. But we haven't talked about the science behind that strength. So how do nature and nurture combine to create Transgenerational Resiliency?

The answer is a combination of epigenetics—literal shifts in our DNA expression—and myelination—the brain's ability to speed up particular thought patterns. Remember, the science of epigenetics tells us that many experiences can change our DNA's expression. In some cases, this shift is passed to the next generation, so that the gift of ancestral strength builds up in our bodies over generations.

And that strength may be expressed through our ability to efficiently restructure our brains. Just as you learned your name as a child, creating the ability to instantly recall that piece of information, we can all train ourselves to be strong in the face of difficult situations. All brains are malleable. All brains restructure throughout their lifetimes. But epigenetics tells us that our bodies are shaped by the previous generations—and that includes our brains.

Thanks to our ancestors, our brains are particularly good at repeating our ancestors' patterns of myelination—at building up the same neural connections that ensured our ancestors' survival.

That doesn't mean that all African Americans are born optimistic. Of course not. Rather, African Americans have inherited an advantage when it comes to myelination. Our brains are well suited to form myelin sheaths around optimistic thoughts—including strength, resiliency, and persistence.

Ken Griffey, Jr. wasn't born playing baseball. But he was born with the proclivity to play baseball. Some of the physical and mental traits that make a good ball player are in his genes.

You might not have been born optimistic. But you were born with generations of ancestral strength in your DNA. Through your ancestors' resiliency, your brain is primed to build strong connections with optimism—to increase your likelihood of finding a resilient, defensive position in the face of difficulty.

That doesn't mean increasing our optimism is easy.

It simply means we *can* do it. And it's all thanks to our ancestors.

THE OPTIMISM CONNECTION: HENRY BOX BROWN

As our brains restructure themselves, they latch onto the things we think about most. Through the magic of epigenetics, African Americans are genetically predisposed to resiliency. But that doesn't mean this generational muscle memory came easily.

Henry Brown was born in 1815, when things were just about as bad as they could be for African Americans. Henry was born in central Virginia to enslaved parents. Forced to work in a tobacco factory, a job of long hours spent on boring tasks, he found some solace in his wife, Nancy. The couple had three children together, although enslaved on different plantations.

But when Nancy was pregnant with their fourth baby, her owner sold her to a plantation in North Carolina. Henry could only watch as hundreds of slaves were marched through the streets in shackles. Among them, his pregnant wife and three small children wept as their chains dragged behind them.

This is not an image of optimism—it's an image of horrible, unthinkable trauma.

For Henry, this experience was the last straw. He could no longer tolerate enslavement. But escape wasn't easy. It took him months of creative thinking. An active member of the First African Baptist Church, he found inspiration in God. His religion helped him to recognize his internal strength and, from there, focus on the things he could control.

As crates of raw tobacco were unloaded from a train one day, Henry imagined climbing aboard, riding the train north until he reached freedom. But enslaved people were heavily guarded. He would almost certainly be caught. The idea nagged at him, though, and he continued to brainstorm ways of hiding himself aboard the rail cars.

And then an idea struck. The trains carried supplies and products through the postal service. Maybe he could mail himself to freedom, he thought.

The idea was crazy, but Henry's optimism persisted. Although his plan was sparked by trauma, he refused to wallow in sadness and anxiety. A close friend of his was a free African American man who associated with white sympathizers. And through his friend, he found just the man to help—an abolitionist named Samuel Smith. Smith found Henry's plan fascinating. While Henry prepared himself mentally for the dangerous—and very likely deadly—undertaking, Samuel purchased a wooden crate.

On March 23, 1849, Henry climbed into a wooden box three feet long, two and a half feet deep, and two feet wide.

It's difficult to imagine the fear he must have felt as Samuel nailed the crate's top in place. With only a small pouch of water and a few dry biscuits, Henry must have known his odds of survival weren't high. But he'd set his mind to resiliency, so he tucked his legs tight to his chest and folded himself into the box while Samuel scrawled "This Side Up" on the top of the crate.

His trip was hellish. At several points during the journey, the box was placed upside down, creating enormous pressure on his head. He described feeling his "eyes swelling as if they would burst from their sockets." After hours spent upside down—just when he thought he might die—he overheard several shipping workers looking for a place to sit down. They chose his box as their impromptu seat, flipping it—and Henry—sideways.

Twenty-seven hours and several shipping transfers later, three Philadelphia abolitionists carefully pried the box open.

"How do you do, Gentlemen?" Henry said, then recited a Bible verse and burst into song.

From then on, he went by the nickname "Box."

Against all odds, he'd escaped slavery. Word spread quickly. The story was too good to keep secret! The men who had helped him escape attempted several more rescues using the same method. But the inspiration of Henry "Box" Brown wasn't so much about the method itself—it was about the possibility of reaching freedom.

In the beginning, his optimism may have seemed unfounded. It may have even seemed foolish. But Henry had two things going for him: epigenetic resiliency and positive myelination.

African Americans had already been enslaved in the United States for generations. So Henry already had the genetic strength of his parents, grandparents, great-grandparents, and other ancestors. Their history multiplied in him to give him the resiliency he needed to persist.

But Henry also had to activate that code. That's where myelination comes in. Through consistently searching for opportunity, he was able to stumble upon an idea so crazy it actually worked. After his wife and children were stolen from him, he might have fallen apart, giving up all hope and waiting to die. Instead, he pursued optimism. He couldn't have known he was going to escape. But he believed in himself, and that belief—combined with his ancestors' remarkable strength—made him truly unstoppable.

HARNESSING GENERATIONAL MUSCLE MEMORY

Your ancestors refused to fail. They survived for you, so that you would be stronger and more resilient. With their persistence in your genes, you can face the toughest obstacles. They also gave you the gift of optimism. Through targeted myelination, you can increase your brain's ability to channel that resiliency.

Later in this book, we'll work through some concrete exercises for leaning into the process of myelination, increasing your optimism, and channeling your ancestors' strategic abilities.

But first, we need to talk about one more tool in the toolbox of brain science: pruning.

CHAPTER 4
MORE THAN WILLING TO THRIVE

FROM THE TRANSATLANTIC slave trade through Jim Crow, segregation, and the other obstacles Black Americans have faced, survival has demanded strength.

Suffering in the cramped lower decks, many abducted Africans never reached America. The sick and the weak died quickly. Healthy captives, too, were susceptible to disease, which spread like wildfire. Many took their own lives. Others were murdered to demonstrate the consequences of resistance.

Of those who made it to the United States—the first African Americans—many didn't survive their working conditions. They died from illness, suicide, malnourishment, and childbirth. Some undoubtedly lost their will to live.

But the strongest remained steadfast, surviving through unthinkably austere conditions. In this impossible environment, only the strong survived. This wasn't just about physical strength, although of course that played a role. Mental stamina—or myelinated resiliency—allowed our amazing ancestors to survive through strength of will.

Those who survived built families and persisted through Jim Crow and segregation, carrying the strength of their ancestors with them. Through epigenetics, they benefitted from generations of resiliency. And through the restructuring brain, they created ironclad connections between adversity and optimism.

It wasn't easy. Far from it.

But they were more than willing to survive—they were willing to *thrive.*

Willingness to thrive is the final piece of the Transgenerational Resiliency puzzle. The psychological ability to persist through adversity, willingness to thrive is about sheer determination.

The physical body needs food, water, and air. It needs medicine and care for injuries.

But thriving through hardship isn't just about the body. It's about the mind. Our bodies' survival demands that our brains *want* to survive. Because when humans lose the will to live, we can—and do—lose our lives as a result.

Psychologists have known this for over a century after a devastating trend emerged in cities along the east coast. In the late nineteenth century, more than one-quarter of New York City's babies died. Henry Chapin was in his late twenties at the time and a newly minted physician. Serving in the poorest areas of the city, he set out to lower infant mortality rates. But first, he had to figure out why the children were dying.

He began by exploring the most obvious potential causes—diets, environmental factors, and disease exposure. None of these explanations fit. He knew he had to find some common factor that united the babies who died. And then it came to him. The infant mortality rate was concentrated within a particular population: orphanages.

At the time, foster care was uncommon, particularly among children who were born poor. Instead, the state placed orphaned babies in group homes. Once they entered the orphanage, children's odds of survival decreased dramatically. Chapin's study explored orphanage mortality rates in ten different cities. With one exception, every institution reported a 100% mortality rate within the first year.

Every infant at these institutions died.

One Baltimore orphanage noted that 10% of infants in their care survived. A horrifying document, their report advanced Chapin's understanding of the tragedy. The orphanage's records revealed a common element among the children who survived: they had all spent time with foster parents.

The children didn't die of starvation, exposure, or disease. They died from a lack of care. Without love, survival was impossible—they simply gave up on life.

Chapin's work offers a powerful lesson for survival through adversity. Without optimism—hope for love, joy, happiness, success—we lose our will to live. This can be deadly for babies. It's harmful to adults, too. Chapin's study changed the government's approach to childcare. Beyond a shadow of a doubt, he proved that willingness to thrive is central to our survival.

MORE THAN WILLING TO THRIVE

Willingness to thrive is a powerful construct that challenges our assumptions about trauma. If we allow ourselves to sink into hopelessness and despair, thriving is impossible. To thrive, we must focus on our strength and persist the way our ancestors did. Early African Americans experienced plenty of trauma. They experienced physical violence, near starvation, emotional abuse, and a level of suffering and loss we can only imagine. But, by restructuring their brains, they learned to persist through trauma without even realizing it. Imagine what it must have been like for early African Americans. Kidnapped from their homes, shackled, and forced into pitch blackness at the bottom of a ship, they must have been terrified. The experience is the very definition of trauma. For years—perhaps the rest of their lives—they may have had nightmares about their kidnapping. They might have even had dissociative reactions, more commonly called flashbacks. When something around them triggered thoughts of the horrendous middle passage—the route from Africa to America—their heart rates probably increased, and their breath probably went shallow.

According to the DSM-5-TR, these are the symptoms of PTSD: intrusive thoughts (nightmares), dissociative reactions (flashbacks), and physiological responses (increased heart rate and breathing). The DSM-5-TR tells us that these symptoms can be completely debilitating, preventing the sufferer from functioning in their day-to-day lives. Today, many people who are diagnosed with PTSD are unable to care for family members, tend to their own homes, or prepare their own meals—much less maintain steady jobs.

Enslaved people didn't have access to mental health diagnoses or treatments. Even if they had, PTSD would not have given them license to miss work.

There isn't much value in a depressed slave, and plantations didn't keep slaves who couldn't perform. No matter how our ancestors felt, they had to get up in the morning and do their work. If they didn't, they risked beatings—or worse.

If they wanted to survive, they had to work through the trauma.

They did this by restructuring their sense of self. Believing deeply in the importance of life, they discovered new strategies and techniques. Without access to medication or therapy, they stabilized their minds and bodies through sheer force of will. That was the only way to keep their lineage alive.

If they'd crumbled in the face of psychological trauma, we would not be here today.

This is the power of willingness to thrive.

To be clear, I'm not arguing that PTSD isn't real. I'm not dismissing the harms of trauma. I'm simply arguing that our ancestors did not have access to care. They had to care for themselves. They did so by restructuring their brains. By restructuring their brains, they altered their DNA's expression. And contemporary African Americans benefit from their ingenuity and determination.

That's Transgenerational Resiliency. Even when we don't realize it, that resiliency is with us, preparing us to thrive in any context. We just have to be willing.

SURVIVAL IN OUR BONES: JESSE OWENS

Jesse Owens was no stranger to difficult contexts. The grandson of an enslaved man and the son of a sharecropper, he struggled through a childhood in the Jim Crow South.

But Owens excelled at athletics. After moving to Ohio, he leaned into his skill in track and field. He broke the high jump record. He crushed the long jump record. And he set an impossible-to-beat speed in the 220-yard dash. In junior high and high school, he racked up win after win, earning him a spot on the Ohio State University's track and field team.

Tragedy nearly struck when Owens fell down a flight of stairs, badly injuring his back. Still, he begged his coach to let him participate in the 1935 Big Ten Championships. One wrong move could lead to further injury, but his coach agreed. They decided that he would participate in the 100-yard dash. The short race would be a trial run. If all went well, Owens would continue to compete in his other events. The starter gun fired and, 9.4 seconds later, Owens crossed the finish line. He'd tied the world record for the event, aching back and all. He achieved three more records that day. With so much success, it's easy to forget that Owens was up against the grueling emotional abuse of racism and segregation. He was treated as a second-class citizen in the United States, despite his powerful athletic prowess. But what he faced in America was just a prelude to his experience in Germany. He traveled to Berlin to compete in the 1936 Olympic Games, a hotbed for the growing Nazi party. Hitler planned to use the Games as propaganda, believing that Aryan athletes would demonstrate the "dominance" of the white race.

But as the games concluded, Owens had taken the podium four times. At his side, Nazis saluted their deadly cause, but Owens stood fast. He was the first American to earn four Olympic gold medals in track and field in a single year, a record that would stand for nearly half a century.

As satisfying as the medals must have been, Owens' performance did more than just earn him the gold—it demonstrated how a willingness to thrive can overcome any psychological barrier. In the face of the extreme torment of Nazi Germany, Owens could have crumbled. He could have declined to attend. In fact, many athletes of color did just that, fearing for their lives and facing pressure from activist groups who hoped to boycott the Games. And then, under Hitler's angry, dismissive gaze, he could have choked.

But he didn't.

He gritted his teeth against Nazi hatred and American racism. He powered through a lifetime of trauma—from his childhood in a state that saw hundreds of lynchings to his college years on a segregated campus. And yet, even with the uncertainty and disappointment racism brings, he found his reason for living. His athletic talent may have been a gift from the generations that came before him. His mental strength certainly was.

Owens was well-known for his stance on politics—he wasn't interested in proving a point; he just wanted to compete. He likely didn't even realize the strength that was in his DNA. But it was there, just the same.

The willingness to thrive is a powerful gift from our ancestors. When we focus on that power, we, like Jesse Owens, become unstoppable.

EXERCISE: LEGACIES OF RESILIENCY

In this exercise, we'll revisit your earlier reflections on your ancestors. Whereas the last exercise asked you to consider the barriers your ancestors faced, this one considers their willingness to thrive. Each of the barriers you identified in the last exercise might have killed your ancestors. But they endured those hardships *for you.* A powerful statement of will, their resiliency is much more important than the barriers they encountered.

In the last exercise, I suggested you talk through your answers with someone you trust. Since this exercise is a continuation of the first, I recommend completing it in the same way. If you chose to write first, do that again. If you gathered information from your family, follow up with them.

The most important thing is that you continue to push your thinking. Let go of any assumptions or preconceived judgments you may hold about your parents, grandparents, or other ancestors. And reflect on their incredible strength—their willingness to thrive.

Answer the following questions, one at a time. Use the bullets below the main questions to help you brainstorm.

Parents

List two or three traits your parents have or had.

If you spent time with your parents as a child, were there things they said or did during difficult times?

How did they make it through life's challenges?

Do you think there were times they wanted to give up?

What stopped them?

Grandparents

Now think about your grandparents. Name a few resilient traits your grandparents have or had.

If they ever told you stories about their lives, how did they tell those stories? Did they incorporate determination, humor, religion, or useful ways of incorporating optimism?

Think about the most difficult event they experienced.

How do you think they got through it?

Do you think there were times they wanted to give up?

What stopped them?

Great-grandparents

What resilient traits did your great-grandparents have?

List two or three.

Put yourself in their shoes. If you were one of their peers, what aspect of society would have been the most difficult for you? How would you have survived it? Do you think that's how they survived it, too?

What gave your great-grandparents the willingness to thrive? What brought them joy, happiness, and hope?

Do you think there were times they wanted to give up?

What stopped them?

Ancestors

Imagine the earliest African Americans. As in the last exercise, try to picture a specific person—someone who was *your ancestor*. List *five* resilient traits you believe your early African American ancestors had.

What do you know about the things your ancestor had to do to survive?

Why do you think they fought so hard to live? What gave them a willingness to thrive even in the face of total oppression?

What pieces of advice might they give you if you could share your struggles with them?

Do you think there were times they wanted to give up?

What stopped them?

Lineage

You should now have a list of fifteen or so total traits. Some may overlap, and that's okay. Now, consider what those traits reveal about the generations that came before you.

Do you see any common themes? Write them down.

Looking at your list of traits, do you see any that you've applied to your life today?

Reflection

Take a moment to consider the things you said and/or wrote. As you move through your day, think about the times when you drew from those resilient traits. You may think of other traits as you continue to reflect on your ancestors. If you do, revisit your list and add those traits for future reference.

Finally, reflect on the following overarching question: What generational traits will you pass on?

EPIGENETICS: KEY POINTS

In this section, I've laid out the basic scientific principles involved in transgenerational resiliency. These ideas form the foundation for the rest of this book, so they're worth reviewing before we move forward to talk about the practical changes you can make in your life to help yourself—and future generations—thrive.

White Psychology

First, white psychology. Most mental health diagnoses and treatments are the results of white scientists studying white participants. This means that many important psychological constructs were created without us in mind.

The most important of these is trauma. Trauma diagnoses often assume that everyone experiences trauma in the same way. However, the prerequisites for being diagnosed with trauma, specifically PTSD, are simply part of the African American experience.

Epigenetics

This leads us to epigenetics. The traumatic events our ancestors survived have never been included in white psychology's discussion of trauma. As a result, our ancestors found ways to navigate these experiences on their own. They did this by developing resiliency.

Epigenetics is the study of how our DNA expression changes throughout our lifetime. Resiliency—the other side of trauma—can have major effects on the way our DNA expresses itself.

Many of these changes are passed through our DNA to the next generation. With each new generation, the expression of resiliency doubles, making contemporary African Americans unstoppable.

Cognitive Restructuring

Epigenetics describes our inherited strength. But we contribute to our own resiliency, too, by restructuring our brains. When we repeatedly retrieve pieces of information—including reactions to particular experiences—our brains protect that information by forming a sheath around the pathway. This is called myelination.

Through epigenetics, African Americans are primed to develop quick-firing optimism. Since our ancestors relied on hope, we are better able to develop it, too.

When we build up our ability to process difficult things through optimism, we are using our ancestors' skills and supplementing those skills with our own practice. This is called generational muscle memory.

Willingness to Thrive

Finally, our ancestors' optimism was a key part of their willingness to thrive.

They endured horrific conditions, but they couldn't sink into depression. They had to keep going. This strength is rooted in their willingness to thrive.

The human body requires more than just basic physiological needs—it also demands a healthy, optimistic outlook. We call this the willingness to thrive, and without it, our bodies cannot excel.

Together, these takeaways demonstrate the incredible power of the African American mind. The strength of our ancestors lives in all of us, whether we recognize it or not. In the next section, I'll teach you to fully realize our ancestors' dreams for your life. The key is cognitive restructuring.

PART TWO

COGNITIVE RESTRUCTURING

CHAPTER 5
TRY, FAIL, PERSIST

"YEAH. WHATEVER," Andre shrugged. He looked down at his hands, picking at something on his index finger. "It's not that bad. Lots of guys go through it."

"What do you mean?" I asked. "You're spending fourteen years in a maximum-security prison. It seems pretty bad to me."

"But then I'll be out."

"And then what?"

He shrugs again, a nervous grin spreading across his face. "I'll figure it out."

I know what he's not saying. What he's not saying is that going to prison was the easy route for him. He'll get through it, day by day, and while he's in here, he'll make new connections with new hustles.

"You can't go back to that," I say. "That's the easy route—going back to what you've always done."

He doesn't look up. I know he doesn't believe me. But I'm used to that, and I'll help him work through it. With his ancestors' strength inside him, he can do anything he sets his mind to. "I get it. There are so many things you don't have control over." I lean forward in the hard plastic chair. "What *can* you control?"

As a forensic psychologist, I work with people like Andre all the time. They're the most optimistic group of people I've ever met. He's in prison because he robbed a house and pawned the jewelry he found. Police easily traced it back to him, and now, here he is—waiting out the clock on a fourteen-year sentence. When he gets out, he thinks, he'll still steal. But he'll be smarter about how he sells stuff. He has total faith in his abilities.

Andre's got optimism for days. He was optimistic that he wouldn't get caught stealing. Now he's optimistic about waiting out the clock. He's optimistic about going back to that life after prison. It makes sense in a way—nobody has any doubt that he can go back to that life if he wants to. It's the easiest path for him, by far.

But he could go a different way. He could read, learn—even get a degree. But that's hard—much harder than waiting out the clock. He could focus on maintaining relationships with his family, even though he's incarcerated. That's hard, too. In this environment, where others make their money through criminal behavior, it's hard to make the decision to find honest work. All of it is so, incredibly difficult.

There are two kinds of optimism. One is simply the confidence that you will survive. The other is a sense of purpose—the feeling that you can grow, learn, and build the best possible life for yourself.

When I first met Andre, he was living day to day. He never doubted that he would make it—after all, survival is in his blood. But as we continued to work together, he found a different kind of optimism. He began to believe that he could make a change in himself. Our ancestors gave us a lot of gifts. We have strength and resiliency in our blood. But we still have to do the work. Like Andre, many of us lean on our old habits. These thought patterns feel easy and comfortable. As long as we lean on our old ways of seeing the world, we have total confidence.

That kind of optimism isn't enough. Our ancestors wanted us to have better lives than they did—we owe it to them to build the best lives possible. Without taking risks—without a willingness to try, fail, and still persist—we will never achieve the lives we deserve.

Changing our habits isn't easy. But with a little work, we can teach our brains to think optimistically; reaching for growth, excellence, and new experiences by default.

The key is cognitive restructuring.

LETTING OUR MINDS WANDER

Every moment in our life either reinforces or dispels our thought patterns, training us to think in particular ways. We rarely realize this is happening. Most of the time, we're too focused on our day-to-day lives to really notice. But each time we see something that matches our worldview, our thought patterns grow stronger. And when we try something new—when something surprises us—our thoughts change.

Therapy sessions—and books like this one—are tools that provide different ways of thinking. As a psychologist, I assist clients in identifying the fallacies in their thought processes. I help separate perceptions from reality. Those perceptions can be stubborn. Even though all of our perceptions are subjective—they are from our point of view alone—they feel very objective. As more personal experiences back up our way of thinking, they grow stronger and stronger until they are indistinguishable from fact. Sometimes that's useful. But most of the time, it just keeps us from growing.

Imagine you wanted to play the piano. If you've never played before, you'd probably struggle at first—a lot. You'd look at the piano keys and have no idea what to do. Staring at the strip of black and white rectangles, you might touch a few keys. But if you tried to play a song, you'd probably fail.

If you learned and practiced, soon you'd know which keys created which sounds. You could easily find the correct note, and you wouldn't be as hesitant to play. After you learned your first song, you'd learn a second and a third. Playing the piano begins as a new set of cognitions, or thoughts. But the more you play, the more the brain reinforces those thoughts. Within a few months, many of those cognitions wouldn't be so new. Years later, the connections would be automatic—myelinated.

But many would-be pianists don't get that far. The reason isn't a lack of talent. It's a different set of cognitions—the voice in our head that tells us we can't. That voice can be very loud, drowning out our goals and ideas. Many of us repeat our failures to ourselves over and over again. We try to play, but the sour notes only reinforce our sense of failure. "Of course, I can't do this. I'm just not musical. I'll never be able to learn." This is a perception that seems factual to the person who says it. In reality, it's nothing but self-sabotage.

Cognitive restructuring retrains our brains, weakening the angry voice in our heads and replacing it with compassion—challenging what we see as facts and reminding us that they are just biased, mean opinions.

Instead of believing we can't play the piano, we can remind ourselves that it's difficult to learn a new instrument. No one is a virtuoso the first time they sit down to play—even Duke Ellington had to learn as a child. He hit a sour note or two, too! And, like Ellington, most early piano players make small improvements in every practice session. If we keep practicing, we can literally hear our own improvement. Take that, negative inner voice!

Just as we can learn to play the piano, we can learn optimism. Rather than looking at new tasks, life changes, or emotional difficulties as impossible, we can understand them as opportunities for growth.

So, what does it take to interrupt the negative voice in our head? How do we replace it with optimism?

One way we can do this is by looking for examples—Duke Ellington, for instance—and reminding ourselves that we can do those things, too.

I saw this firsthand with my kids. When my son was a small child in the early 2000s, he asked me what he would be when he grew up. I turned the question back to him.

"What do you *want* to be when you grow up?"

"I don't know..."

"You can be anything you want to be," I told him. "Except,

maybe, president. We've never had an African American president, so that would be harder."

"But I can be anything else?"

"Yep!"

I'm sure you can see where this is going. My younger son was born in 2009. Barack Obama was president. By then, my oldest had a better sense of whom he wanted to be. Our conversations had changed from the concerns of a child to those of an adolescent, and he was much more interested in friends and girls than his vocational future.

But my younger son wanted to know what he would be when he grew up, too. And this time, I had a different answer. Obama's election had changed the landscape of our country, at least in terms of the possibilities for young African American dreamers, and it had changed my cognitions, too. I'd spent years thinking of the presidency as something that was reserved for white men. Now, through Obama's example, I could imagine a different future. My previous experiences—three decades of them—told me that African Americans could not serve in the highest office in the country.

Just one example proved me wrong.

Just one example gave me—and my sons—optimism.

THE FAILS METHOD

Optimistic thinking is not about ignoring the bad things in our lives. Everyone experiences hardships and failures. Optimism is about taking those hardships and failures and turning them into opportunities for growth.

Because true optimism requires us to try, fail, and persist, I developed an approach to cognitive restructuring called the FAILS method. A military-based approach, this method helped Andre, and I use it in my own life, too. It's not easy, but it is simple.

The FAILS acronym stands for:

Focus on your power

Accept what you can't control
Isolate problems in their proper area
Learn to grow
Share good news

Through these five steps, any problem can become a source of optimism. That was certainly true for my client, David.

When I first met David, he was struggling at work. A reception clerk at a large hotel, he'd always loved his job: the schedule was predictable, the customers were interesting, and his coworkers were friendly. Best of all, his shift ended just in time to pick up his daughter. He'd leave the hotel, drive across town, and arrive at the school just as Camisha's gap-toothed grin appeared in the preschool's doorway. But when a new manager replaced his old boss, things changed. The new manager often expected employees to stay past their shifts. Now, he often found himself racing across town, cursing at traffic all the way. By the time he got there, Camisha would be the last child waiting. The glares of the preschool teachers were the cherry on top of his bad luck. During his precious time with his daughter, he often found himself stewing over the unfairness of the situation, unable to focus on anything but his frustration.

I encouraged David to communicate with his new boss, offering to come in early if he was allowed to leave on time. He agreed, but David's problems persisted. Now it wasn't his boss who expected him to stay late—it was a coworker. She would grumble under her breath and make snide comments about him leaving "early." Just as frustrated by her judgment as he was by the traffic, David still found that he couldn't relax after work. He was growing resentful of his workplace for making him feel this way, and he felt ashamed that he sometimes took his frustrations out on Camisha.

Over time, I worked with David to practice the FAILS method. First, he had to Focus on the power he had in the situation. There was nothing he could do about his coworker's attitude. But he did have the power to ignore her. The only thing he could really control was his emotional state.

This took him to the next stage: Accepting what he could not control.

David decided to work on a positive mindset. Reminding himself of what his ancestors endured, he realized that a few snarky comments didn't matter much in the long run. His coworker could say whatever she wanted. He couldn't stop her—he could only control how he reacted. Accepting what he did—and did not—have power over shifted his focus, ultimately leading him to feel happier and more empowered. Focus and Acceptance were a good start, but David was also struggling to keep his work life from affecting his family life. Here's where Isolation comes in. Whenever David felt tempted to carry his annoyance out of the office and all the way to Camisha's preschool, he refocused his thoughts—instead of giving brain space to his coworker, he focused on the fun things he could do with his daughter when they got home. Maybe they could take a walk or go to the park. Maybe they could watch Frozen for the seven-hundredth time. Maybe they could read a book together or draw a picture. Having these thoughts ready gave him something positive to think about—and it made him even more excited for his family time.

Within a relatively short time, David was feeling better about work. His coworker continued to make little jabs under her breath, but more and more David found that they didn't bother him. At this point, I pushed him to think about what he'd Learned. Some days, he still felt frustrated. But now, his annoyance taught him something—just for that day, he hadn't succeeded at Focusing, Accepting, and Isolating. An opportunity to learn, his failure became a data point. He could think about what had happened that day, and why it undercut his efforts. And, once he knew why he'd failed, he could improve even more.

Along the way, David experienced a lot of little successes and failures. While our failures can teach us to refocus and build new strategies, our successes can reinforce our learning. A few months into practicing the FAILS method, David finally felt control over his emotions, keeping his cool in the workplace and at home. I encouraged him to share his success with others.

The next week, David shared a conversation he'd had at a t-ball game. While chatting with another parent, he told her about the FAILS method and how it had helped him. Impressed, she'd asked him to write it down so she could practice herself. This was a huge confidence booster for David. He'd accomplished something difficult, and sharing his success helped him celebrate his win! We Share our successes because doing so helps us build confidence. It gives us a boost of dopamine—the chemical that makes us feel warm and fuzzy. This tells the brain to keep up the good work and encourages it to myelinate our practiced optimism. Ultimately making our outlook unbreakable.

David realized we have the power to control our emotions and our responses. We can't control others. We can't control our environment. We can't control society. But we can control how we react to others—we *can* control our outlook.

David embraced the FAILS method, and eventually found himself much more optimistic in his everyday life. He no longer talked about his obligation to pick up Camisha from school. Now he talked about his opportunity to pick her up, something that not all dads get to do!

The method not only improved his outlook at work. It also helped him to be more optimistic throughout his life. And the FAILS method is so easy and versatile that it can work for any problem, large or small.

EXERCISE: INCREASING YOUR OPTIMISM

In this exercise, you'll practice using the FAILS method in your own life. As with all exercises, I recommend that you write down your answers and share them with a trusted friend, family member, or therapist. It can be helpful to get an outside perspective on the issue, particularly if you are struggling to find optimism in your responses.

The most important thing is that you remember the strength you have in your DNA. Your ancestors did hard things so that you would have the strength and resiliency to persist. Go out and make them proud!

To practice this method, let's begin by considering a problem at work. Perhaps you have a difficult boss or coworker. Or maybe you're having trouble finding a job. Maybe the commute is frustrating, or your hours aren't ideal. If you're a stay-at-home caregiver, you might struggle with isolation or feel your efforts aren't recognized. Or, if you're a student, you might find a particular subject or teacher difficult. All of these can fall under the umbrella of our work life. The important thing is choosing a single problem.

Identify A Problem

First, write down the problem in a single sentence.

You've probably got a lot more to say about the issue. When we're frustrated and upset, our thoughts can run on overdrive. So it's crucial to stick to a single problem and push yourself to keep it short and simple.

Now, let's use the FAILS method to find the optimism in the situation.

Focus On Your Power

Look back at your problem sentence. How could you reword it as an opportunity?

Where do you have power in the situation?

David had to search hard for his power, but it was always there—he had the power to ignore his coworker and enjoy his life. Where do you have control in your own situation? Write it down.

Accept What You Can't Control

This next step can be challenging, but it's incredibly freeing. Look back at your original problem sentence. What aspects of the sentence are *beyond your control*? Write them down.

How might you approach those aspects with acceptance? How can you reframe them in a way that allows you to accept them as small bumps in the road?

Isolate Problems

This third step can be the most difficult. By isolating problems, we keep them from bleeding into all aspects of our lives. Practicing this step keeps us from ruminating over things, which ultimately saves us from accidentally myelinating the bad.

David's problem invaded his entire life, bleeding into his family time. He chose to counter those thoughts by planning fun activities with his daughter.

Think of one time when you were unable to shut out the bad thoughts—when you found your work problem following you home.

What thoughts could you have used to replace the problem thoughts?

How can you redirect your brain in the future to focus on your home life? Write down several specific ideas.

Learn to Grow

Growing is about more than just mindset—it's about action. The next phase of the FAILS model asks us to consider how we might grow from both the positives and the negatives. This increases optimism by turning everything we encounter into an opportunity for growth. When we struggle, we can grow by figuring out concrete actions and using available resources. When we face a difficult choice, we can grow by being bold and taking reasonable risks. And when we fail, we can evaluate what went wrong so that we can move forward with even more confidence. David had to mess up more than a few times before he achieved his goal. But remember, he saw his failures as opportunities to learn and grow.

What failures have you experienced as you've tried to work through your workplace stressor?

What have you tried that just didn't work? How have you learned from this problem?

Remember that failures are just data points. Write down a few strategies you've tried. Now brainstorm some new approaches that might work better.

Share Good News

This is really the fun part! You won't conquer your problem immediately, but if you focus on the FAILS method and optimistic thinking, you'll see small changes almost immediately. Don't keep them to yourself—share them with others. These small achievements are worth celebrating! They make us feel happier and more optimistic, which is the key to tapping into our ancestors' strength.

David shared his success with another parent. It helped her improve her own situation and gave him a huge confidence boost!

Write down a few ways you can share and celebrate your growth.

EMBRACING FAILURE

The FAILS method works with any problem you encounter—workplace tensions, family struggles, relationship issues, and financial constraints all benefit from this method. As we try, fail, and persist, we build up our confidence and sense of optimism.

And, as we'll discuss in the next chapter, optimism is the best antidote for anxiety.

CHAPTER 6
UNTANGLING THE ANXIETY LOOP

THE TWO PLAYERS stared at each other across the board, sizing up one another and planning for their next strategic moves. When it was her turn, the black player shifted her pawn forward one space. The white player countered, fatally sliding the bishop in one, smooth diagonal sweep.

That move prepared the black queen for victory, her player shuffling the rounded piece onto a winning space. The black queen had secured yet another conquest.

Key to this game, the black queen is the most powerful piece on the board. She can move in any direction, her capabilities limited only by the number of squares she can travel. With free range of movement, the black queen places immense pressure on her opponents.

She's a force to be reckoned with—a looming piece with no fear or uncertainty. She moves across the board with purpose and intention, exercising her will to win. The black queen is the most feared piece on the chessboard, and rightfully so. Her power is unmatched. With the black queen on your side, you have a fighting chance against anyone.

That's not just a matter of chance. In the game of chess, the white side always moves first. This gives them the advantage of beginning on the offensive—they get to attack before they ever have to defend themselves. The black side, on the other hand, must begin by fending off the white player's first move.

In a mismatched game—or a game in which the initial strategy fails—the black player may never get to play offense. Stuck in a cycle of batting down each new threat, the black player spends all their energy worrying. And all that fear prevents them from focusing on the win.

This isn't just a description of the moves in a game of chess. It's also a powerful metaphor for understanding how epigenetic power serves African Americans in our daily lives. Our ancestors navigated crushing moments of racism, discrimination, violence, and murder, but still emerged stronger than ever. Just like the best chess players, they had to watch the whole board. Lined up in eight columns of eight rows each, the chess board is complex and intimidating—and so were the threats that faced our ancestors.

And even when they felt completely outmatched in the face of white racism, they had to keep their chins up and their shoulders back, trusting that the strength of their ancestors would guide them through even the most difficult times.

Now, like the black queen, we've been given the resiliency to navigate our world, too.

The chess board tells us something else, too—it tells us that success is all about strategy. A model for all of us as we navigate our lives, the skills needed in chess are about finesse, care, awareness, and hidden power.

It's no wonder the black queen is the most powerful piece in the game. Mirroring her, African American women are our superheroes, playing a vital and unstoppable role in facilitating our cultural growth. In chess, the queen can mirror all other pieces' moves, apart from the knight. This is analogous to the multifaceted roles of African American women in society. From raising children to leading communities and being foundational support for African American communities, they have always been an essential piece of our culture. In turn, unlike the white queen in a game of chess who has the privilege of moving first, the black queen must play defense as well as offense. She has the resiliency to withstand these attacks, but she knows how to spot weaknesses. She knows how to exploit them.

African Americans have always had to use these psychological tools to survive and thrive. We've always had to be focused, fearless, strategic, and smart. We mature early, since the black queen's influence in our lives helps us endure hardship without breaking. We learn to take hardship as an opportunity, taught to us very young and embedded in our DNA. This invisible power is the reason African Americans have been able to persist and become powerful figures in society today. We've always had to be optimists—the alternative is simply not an option.

Whether or not you play chess, the game offers a powerful metaphor for transgenerational resiliency. Not only does the game take years—even decades—to perfect; it also shows us that we must step back to see the entire board in order to make informed decisions about our next moves. If we focus on just one pawn, it's easy to feel as though we can't predict the game.

But chess masters will tell you that, if we look at the whole board, we can—and must—focus several steps ahead of the current move at hand.

Chess is a game of patterns. So is life.

By thinking of history as a chess board, we remind ourselves of recurring—or, in other words, predictable—strategies and tactics. We identify the reliable patterns of African American resiliency and anticipate the barriers that have blocked our ancestors for centuries.

Anxiety arises when we don't know what to expect. So searching for patterns in our world and in ourselves is the surest way to embrace our inner resiliency and untangle the anxiety loop.

THE ANXIETY LOOP

Derrick had been working as a customer service operator for years, but he dreamed of a promotion to management. He'd built up his resume, worked hard to develop leadership skills, and always showed up on time, ready to work. When the head of client relations retired one year, his immediate supervisor was promoted, and Derrick was invited to apply for the management position. He loved his company —his coworkers were friendly, the pay rates were fair, and the benefits were competitive—this was truly his dream job.

So, naturally, the evening before the interview, he felt anxious. He couldn't stop thinking about what an important step this was in his career, and how disappointed he would be if he didn't get the job.

As he and his wife watched their evening Netflix, he realized his palms were sweating. His heart beat fast, and he found he couldn't concentrate on the show. Although he didn't realize it, his blood pressure had risen, an undetectable physiological sign that signaled to his body and brain that a threat was on the horizon.

"You okay?" his wife asked.

"Yeah," he replied. "Just nervous."

She smiled and nodded encouragingly. "You'll do great, baby. I have total faith in you!"

But her words didn't help. He couldn't sleep that night, tossing and turning as he worried about the next day's events. And, like clockwork, he felt exhausted when the morning came.

Inside, his mind churned with negative thoughts.

What if I don't know the answer to a question?

Why didn't I practice more?

What if I trip on the garbage can on the way into the office?

Is my suit wrinkled?

Are my sweaty underarms showing?

What if I make a complete fool of myself?

Focused on his anxiety, Derrick couldn't think about anything else—his mind continually returned to the pit in his stomach. And it wasn't just the interview—he realized that he even had anxiety about his anxiety. The more he thought about it, the more panicked he felt.

No matter how hard he tried, he couldn't seem to stop himself from worrying.

By the time lunch rolled around, Derrick was seriously considering skipping the interview. He called his wife to run the idea by her.

"What?! Why?!" she asked. "I mean, I'll support you no matter what, but I thought you were excited about this job!"

"I just don't think I'll get it anyway. What's the point of embarrassing myself if there's no chance?"

"Derrick," she said. "They invited you to apply. They obviously want to consider you."

"Maybe. But we don't know how many other people they invited. It probably makes more sense to just pick up a few double shifts and make some extra money that way."

Derrick's anxiety was out of control. Internalizing it, he shut off his natural resiliency and allowed his mind to spiral. From our outside perspective, Derrick looks almost silly. None of his fears were true, and, as his wife pointed out, his company seemed excited to consider him for the new position. None of that matters when we find ourselves in the middle of an anxiety loop.

When we focus on our anxiety, it only gets worse. And the more we try to break out of the loop, the harder it becomes. The anxiety loop is a self-defeating, self-sabotaging cycle that only heightens our anxiety. It's maladaptive and unhealthy, and it keeps us from living our best lives.

For some of us, anxiety can be completely debilitating. Once we fall into the anxiety loop, we struggle to function in our everyday lives. We might miss work, cancel social plans, and withdraw from activities we once enjoyed. The anxiety loop can have a serious impact on our mental and physical health as well as our relationships, careers, and goals.

That's because anxiety is essentially a fear of the future—and the future is unknowable. We worry about potential negative outcomes, and that worry leads to anxiety in the present. People often describe uncertainty as a major trigger for their anxiety: they're anxious because they don't know what will happen.

This is precisely the problem! Anxiety isn't about a real event. Often, it isn't even about real possibilities. Anxiety is about our perception of the future—a product of our own minds.

The good news is that our ancestors left us tools to untangle the anxiety loop. They've left us more than capable of controlling our anxiety to find peace and calm in the present moment.

The reason, perhaps ironically, is the future. African Americans have always had hope for the future. As we've discussed in previous chapters, our ancestors could not have survived without hope.

But hope is not the same as certainty.

Our ancestors had hope, but they rarely knew what lay ahead. Like jumping out of a plane and praying your parachute opens, they didn't know what would happen when they took that step. But they knew in their genes—even if not in their conscious minds—that their next move was going to make things better. One step at a time, they kept moving forward—from slavery, from lynching, from segregation.

While the future isn't certain, the past is. We can look to history to see how hundreds of years of reinforcement formed genes so strong that they're unbreakable. We can directly observe the mental toughness in our ancestors and know, for certain, that it's in us, too.

That's optimism. And we now know we can myelinate optimism, ensuring that the conscious side of resiliency is always at our fingertips, ready when we need it to soothe our fears.

Once we access our innate optimism and resiliency, anxiety isn't a problem. When we're optimistic, we don't fear failure. When we're optimistic, we know—even if we can't see it yet—things will work out.

And, in a way, that's certainty.

When we're caught in the anxiety loop, it's because we've lost sight of our optimism. We've allowed our anxiety to take over and steal our ability to think clearly. But we can break out of the anxiety loop by reconnecting with our optimism.

Optimism—particularly myelinated optimism—is like a pair of sharp sheers to an anxiety loop. And we can snip that loop open and escape if we keep our eyes on our ancestors.

It's not always easy, but it is possible. And it's worth it. When we're free from anxiety, we're free to live our best lives.

COGNITIVE RESTRUCTURING: THE KEY TO ESCAPING ANXIETY

The most enlightening experience I've had when it comes to anxiety loops happened during my tour in Africa. At one point during my time there, my group had to speak with a powerful African leader.

Although I wasn't high ranking, the leader gravitated to me, the only African American in the group. He refused to speak to my white sergeant, choosing to communicate only with me.

This annoyed my white leader, who felt that the African leader should be forced to speak with him, whether he wanted to or not. In fact, my sergeant even told the mission's commander that he wouldn't work with me if I continued to allow the African leader to communicate through me.

But of course, I didn't have control over the African leader, and neither did my sergeant. Calm and cool, the African leader stood his ground, preferring to speak to a Black private rather than a higher-ranking white officer. Our commander saw that. He told my sergeant to make it work—although I imagine his language was somewhat more colorful—and my sergeant did.

By standing their ground, the Africans showed us, beyond a shadow of a doubt, that they were the ones who had the power.

I wasn't a psychologist then, but I've always been fascinated by the power of the human mind, so I took some time to observe the Africans' behavior. They valued things differently than we did. They understood the power of trust—of believing that everything would work out. And they held steadfast in that belief.

The Africans frequently used the phrase, "God willing"—"We'll meet tomorrow, God willing." "We'll complete the project next month, God willing." "Our countries will work together, God willing."

They knew they couldn't see the future, but they trusted that things would work out the way they were meant to.

They had to. For their villages to function, they often sent young girls to fetch water, walking barefoot for five miles on their own. These children showed no fear, even though some of them must have been as young as three or four years old. "If God wants me back," they believed, "I'll be back."

While many Americans might shudder at the thought—imagining a lion or tiger springing from the bushes to devour their child—neither the children nor their parents showed that fear. They had learned to identify which things they could control and, perhaps more importantly, which things they couldn't.

One day, we joined the Africans on a patrol. Suddenly a pack of wild boars appeared in the distance. Some of the Americans aimed their rifles at the animals. Others stood frozen.

But the Africans quickly scaled the surrounding trees.

"Get up here," they said. "That's not a battle worth fighting."

That type of optimism is key to survival. It's not always about force. It's about strategy. It's about trusting that the right thing will happen and then letting go of our need for control. It's that need for control—the desire for certainty—that makes us anxious.

The more desperately we cling to our need for certainty, the more anxiety sets in. And the more anxiety sets in, the more cyclical it becomes until it forms a seemingly unbreakable loop in our minds.

The Africans were able to think quickly, moving through the forest and to fearlessly sending their kids to haul water because that's how they'd been taught to see the world. Since they were small children, they practiced optimism and trust until the two ideas became unbreakably connected, instilled in their very being.

For most of us, that connection isn't as strong. But we know we can build up that connection through cognitive restructuring.

What if I asked you not to think about a tiger? Most of us would immediately picture a tiger.

That's because it's nearly impossible to not think about something.

Instead, we need to replace the harmful thoughts—anxiety—with the thoughts that serve us—optimism. If African children focused on not thinking about a tiger, two things would happen: first, they would likely experience much more anxiety, and second, their anxiety would prevent them from spotting dangerous predators. So caught up in their own mind, their internalized anxiety would become a bigger threat than the actual animals around them.

Instead of not thinking about a tiger, African school children think about optimism. They focus on the opportunity to go to school, the availability of fresh water, or the good they are doing for their families and villages. They focus on positive aspects of their lives. That doesn't mean they ignore the dangers—they still run up a tree when they see a pack of wild boars coming! But since they are socialized from birth to trust the will of the universe, they don't get trapped in anxiety loops that only end up harming them.

If you, like me, weren't taught this approach as a child, it might not come so easily to you. Learning to trust that everything will work out—that we are resilient and strong—can take some practice. It requires us to repeatedly focus on our resiliency until we achieve a strong, myelinated connection between threatening aspects of our environment—from job interviews to tigers—and the optimism of our ancestors.

Myelination isn't easy. As we've discussed previously, it takes repeated practice to ensure that optimism is our first instinct. Our ancestors created that ability in us, and with a little trust, we can tap into our epigenetic powers of resiliency.

REPLACING ANXIETY WITH OPTIMISM

In this chapter, I highlighted the power of the anxiety loop. Once our brains get trapped in the cycle of fear, it can be very difficult to free ourselves. If we don't stop the anxiety loop—ideally before it begins—then we find ourselves spiraling.

Therefore, it's so important to think about our power. Like the black queen in chess, we are powerful. We are strong. We are resilient. But if we place all our focus on defensive strategies, we forget to look for positive opportunities. Like Derrick, we end up sabotaging our own efforts because we listen to that fearful, anxious voice in our heads.

With our ancestors' help, we can crush the anxiety loop every time. The next chapter will show you how.

CHAPTER 7
THE PARADOX OF SUFFERING

BOOT CAMP IS GRUELING. The most difficult part—at least at first—is getting up early in the morning to run. At the crack of dawn, an instructor would come into our barracks and shout at us to wake up. We were often dead asleep, and the yelling would scare us nearly out of our skin.

Still stunned from being startled awake like that, we had to run. They'd yell then, too. "Move faster!" They peppered many of their commands with curse words and personal insults. "Run, run, run."

In those moments, I could feel my central nervous system going into overdrive. Adrenaline coursed through my body, straight to my legs. I don't know how, but somehow we all managed to put one foot in front of the other.

Our nervous systems are automatic. We can learn to restructure our brains, but our initial responses occur without our direct consent. Our sympathetic nervous system, in particular, is prone to automatic firing, leading some people to call this our reptilian brain. This is the part of the brain that tells us to panic or flee when we are afraid, the part that makes us feel warm and fuzzy when we hold a baby, and the part that makes our stomach turn when we smell something rotten.

My reptilian brain went into overdrive the first few times I woke up to an instructor screaming—maybe more than just the first few if I'm being honest. Coursing through my body and sending my mind reeling, the fear response flowed through my body. My thoughts, if you can call them that, flew too fast to process, and my body moved automatically.

This went on morning after morning until, one day, I wasn't so scared. One day, I woke up before he came in to yell at us. The wake-up call sounded less like angry shouting and more like motivation. I knew what to do, and it was time to do it. And as I ran, I felt less frightened and more exhilarated. I didn't realize it then, but my parasympathetic nervous system was kicking in—telling my body to relax and conserve its energy for a real threat. My mind eventually learned what to expect. The connection between the instructors and my feet pounding against the pavement became myelinated. Even though running wasn't always fun—sometimes we were deeply exhausted, sometimes it was raining or hot, and sometimes we just wanted a day off—I knew I could do it. I'd done it before, and I knew I would do it again.

Even something as tough as boot camp helped me to develop optimism in a part of my life. In some ways, it may seem paradoxical. We often think of the most difficult things in our lives as just that —difficult.

But when we realize that suffering through hard times can make us stronger, we literally change our minds. Those early morning runs didn't hurt me, no matter how hard they felt at the time. They made me stronger. The more I realized this, the more confident I became.

This is the paradox of suffering—when we struggle through hardships, we learn that we can achieve anything. Our nervous systems let go of their instinctive fear response, and our brains rewire themselves to answer familiar hardships with optimism.

When we think of it this way, suffering is a privilege. Before anyone closes this book, let me explain what I mean.

Even though suffering itself is, by definition, awful, when we undergo things that threaten to kill us, we learn more about our strength. And not just consciously. Our brains rewire themselves when we live through the unthinkable. With true suffering in mind, our brains create a sense of scale. After months of boot camp, my home alarm clock and early morning gym routine seemed too minor to complain about. Finally back home, at least I was sleeping in my own bed. I could grab a cup of coffee on the way to the gym. My wife and I could even go together. Experiencing the suffering of boot camp showed me that most of my everyday struggles were hardly struggles at all. I'd achieved one of the hardest things I'd ever done—I passed with flying colors, in fact—I could achieve anything!

One of the most powerful aspects of transgenerational resiliency is that we don't even have to complete the suffering ourselves. With the gifts of our ancestors, we can understand resiliency through them, inheriting the strength they gained from suffering. We can reflect on the terrible things our ancestors lived through and, like my time in boot camp, form a shell of protection around ourselves. When we're protected by our ancestors' psychological resiliency—like an armor around our bodies and minds—nothing can stop us.

THE ARMOR OF PSYCHOLOGICAL RESIDUE

The key to understanding the paradox of suffering is psychological residue. Psychological residue is the emotional stuff that sticks to our brains after we experience major events in our lives. Neither good nor bad, psychological residue is just part of life.

Most of us have experienced something we would describe as life-changing. For example, I'll never forget the first time I held each of my children. If you've got kids, you understand. Something changes inside you at that moment, and you know you'll never think of love the same way again.

If you've experienced a profound loss—perhaps the death of a loved one—you know that the grief lingers within you. While it changes and lessens over time, it can still leap out at you, unexpectedly, pulling you right back into your pain. That kind of grief never really leaves us.

These are both examples of psychological residue.

Just as we all have different experiences, we all have different forms of residue. But all of us have our psychological residue to shape our responses to future interactions. People often change their priorities after the birth of a baby or the death of a family member. That's psychological residue lingering in the body, preparing for the next big event.

When we think of things this way, the paradox of suffering becomes clear. Everyone experiences traumatic things. Suffering is universal. But how we look at it can affect how it's stored in our bodies and minds. Dwelling on our losses—allowing them to form anxiety loops, for example—can create a harmful residue that tells us to shy away from hard things. But if we remind ourselves of our optimism, we can create positive residue in ourselves, even through suffering.

Boot camp wasn't the only difficult part of being in the military. As a member of our military, I saw some terrible things. Those things were traumatic, especially if we rely on White Psychology's definition of trauma. But I took those moments as growth opportunities. I looked at them as a way to learn about my surroundings, evaluate my team members, and find my inner strength.

The residue of those experiences became my armor.

Residue stays with us. It changes us. And while some psychological residue can hold us back, with cognitive restructuring, we can emerge from difficulties even stronger than before. Part of that work involves forging an optimistic connection that draws from our suffering.

PRODUCTIVE OPTIMISM, NOT ENTITLEMENT

My wife invited a couple of her friends over for drinks. Jada and Ashley were just finishing up their nursing degrees. They were stressed because they needed jobs—and some of the openings pitted them against each other. They both had children—my wife met Jada during a childbirth class—and both were in their early forties. With similar educational backgrounds and speech styles, Jada and Ashley were nearly identical job candidates.

The only difference was their race. Jada is African American, while Ashley is white.

I brought the open bottle of pinot grigio to where they sat in the living room and refilled each of their glasses.

"Joe," Ashley said, a little tipsy. "Why is it so hard to find a good job?"

I shrugged, trying to stay out of the conversation, but Ashley persisted.

"It's just impossible to get anybody to hire me. I'm a mom—they hate hiring moms. And already in my forties. Strike two."

I glanced over at my wife and Jada. Her face unreadable, my wife took a sip of her wine. Jada chewed her lip.

"Those are silly reasons not to hire somebody," I said.

"I know!"

"What about you, Jada. Any luck?"

At that, Jada's face lit up. "Yep! I just accepted a position at the east campus."Ashley looked hurt, so she added, "You'll find something, too, Ash!"

"How many jobs did you guys apply for?" I asked. I was wearing out my welcome, but the group dynamic was interesting, and I sensed that something more was happening under the surface.

"Just one," Ashley said. She took a big gulp of her wine. "I fit every single requirement on their list. Nothing. Just ghosted me. I'm telling you—I was *perfect* for this job!!"

I gave her a sympathetic look. "Did you just apply to one, too?" I asked Jada.

She shook her head and held up four fingers.

Nodding, I excused myself from the group, but I couldn't shake the sense that Jada's psychological residue had prepared her in a way that Ashley couldn't have imagined.

As a Black woman, Jada has experienced a lot of difficulties in her life. She realized that employment discrimination is alive and well in America, so she applied for four different jobs in the beginning.

Ashley hadn't lived any of this. She'd experienced some hardships in her life—everyone has. But her privilege left her vulnerable to the realities of the job market.

This is psychological residue. From years of racism, Jada developed an armor of suffering. She remained optimistic—always believing she would find a job—but she also knew she needed to apply for several. So, she shook off the rejections, tossing the letters in the recycling bin and preparing for her next interview.

Ashley, on the other hand, was deeply bothered by the jobs she didn't get. She came up with every excuse, every reason they didn't hire her, forgetting that Jada shared every single one of those traits with her. Having experienced very few hardships based on her identity and appearance, Ashley was simply unprepared for disappointment. Without the armor of residue, she was left fragile and hurt.

Jada and Ashley are both optimistic people. But for Ashley, optimism looks a lot like entitlement—because she was qualified for the job, she believed it was owed to her. She'd never been rejected, and, with that life experience in mind, she couldn't imagine being turned away. That type of optimism can only take us so far. It will never develop into strength and resiliency because it's based on faulty assumptions about the world.

Jada's optimism, on the other hand, is rooted in her previous experiences of suffering. She's always come out okay, but she expects a few bumps along the road. That's why she applied to four jobs when Ashley only applied to one. And if she hadn't gotten any of those jobs, I'm willing to bet she would have kept applying until she did. She had the psychological residue to persist, even though it meant shrugging off rejections along the way.

But how do we ensure that our psychological residue becomes

optimistic armor rather than debilitating anxiety? How do we avoid adopting entitlement like Ashley and, instead, maintain our optimism like Jada?

The key is to consciously shift our thoughts. By altering our thoughts, we change our moods. This leads to better actions and more ideal behaviors.

EXERCISE: RESTRUCTURING YOUR APPROACH

To ensure that our optimism is as productive as possible, we can turn to the cycle of thoughts, moods, actions, and behaviors. When we think realistic but optimistic thoughts, we boost our mood. The positive energy we gain from our mood can then encourage us to take productive physical actions. When those actions become behaviors—or habits—we have started to change our lives for the better, leading to even more positive thinking.

This is the process of turning suffering into a privilege.

In this exercise, you'll develop a set of images that will help you remind yourself to trust in your psychological residue. This exercise benefits from writing down or drawing your responses, so make sure you have a sheet of paper handy before you begin. Feel free to step away from the exercise and come back to it later. Some of the things you'll consider might require a bit more thought, and that's okay.

We can think of thoughts, moods, actions, and behaviors as four pieces of a pie. This exercise will lead you through creating salient images for each of the four quadrants, allowing you to redirect your thoughts whenever you feel yourself sinking into entitlement or negativity.

Begin by brainstorming answers for each of the following questions.

Thoughts

Thinking about the lessons you've learned from this book so far, what are some positive thoughts you have about your ancestors?

What positive psychological, emotional, intellectual, or physical traits have you inherited from previous generations of your family?

Where do you see generational resiliency in your bloodline?

What skill, mindset, or achievement makes you your ancestors' wildest dreams?

Moods

How would you describe your mood on a day when you feel like you can accomplish anything you put your mind to? What kind of mood do you like to achieve in the mornings? What kind of mood do you prefer in the evenings? What about on your days off?

If a parent or grandparent were to brag about you to a friend, how would they describe your mood or attitude?

What feeling do you get when you finally reach a goal?

Actions

When you want to feel your best, what do you physically do?

What is one thing you could do for yourself this week to boost your mood?

If you wanted to improve your relationship with someone you care about—a friend, family member, or significant other—what would you do?

What bit of advice have you heard that you know you should do, but just haven't gotten around to?

Behaviors

What habits could you form to feel healthier and happier, physically, mentally, emotionally, or otherwise?

How can you remind yourself to do one positive thing for yourself every week?

What behaviors are you doing when you really feel good about yourself?

What can you do in your day-to-day life to remind yourself of your transgenerational resiliency and emotional armor?

Reflection

Once you've completed all the questions in the four quadrants, look back at your answers. From each of the lists you made, choose one key answer that you believe will have the biggest impact. On your sheet of scratch paper, draw a circle and divide it into four equal pieces by drawing one horizontal line and one vertical line. In the top left quadrant, write the one answer you chose from the "Thoughts" list above. Keep it concise so you can read it at a glance.

In the top right quadrant, list your key answer from the "Moods" question.

Write your "Action" answer in the bottom right quadrant, and your "Behaviors" answer in the bottom left quadrant.

This is your map to effective cognitive restructuring. By looking at your circle, you can remind yourself of the person you want to be. If you realize you've gone off course, you can remind yourself by using your chosen thought pattern. When you're in a bad mood, use the answer you wrote in that section. Actions can be helpful if you find yourself going off course or falling into the anxiety loop. And, finally, Behaviors will help you remember the everyday habits you want to form to become a more optimistic and resilient person.

Tape your map to your bathroom mirror, inside your car, or near your computer—somewhere you'll see it almost every day. Each time you enter that space, review your chosen cycle of optimism, including the four answers on your map, and keep trying, failing, and persisting until you notice your life changing for the better.

COGNITIVE RESTRUCTURING: KEY POINTS

This section has introduced you to the primary tool of psychotherapy: cognitive restructuring. Although our ancestors left us powerful armor in our DNA, we still must help ourselves by using our minds to their fullest potential.

Let's review what we've learned in this section.

The FAILS Method

The FAILS method stands for Focus, Accept, Isolate, Learn, and Share. This method allows us to shift our everyday thinking by identifying the weaknesses in negative thoughts. By homing in on the things we can control—and by keeping our work struggles at work and our home struggles at home—we empower ourselves to do the difficult, but necessary work to make our lives better.

The Anxiety Loop

The anxiety loop occurs when our minds cycle through negative thoughts over and over. Eventually, we begin to focus on our fears and the discomfort that comes from being afraid.

Anxiety comes from uncertainty about the unknown. To combat this, we can remind ourselves that one thing is always certain: we will be okay. This is how our ancestors survived, and it's how we will get through the tough times too.

The Paradox of Suffering

The tough times can even help us, especially when we remember the paradox of suffering.

When we are frightened, overwhelmed, or stressed, our sympathetic nervous systems take over. These reptilian brains act on their own, moving so quickly we have no time to process our emotions, let alone generate a plan to save ourselves.

But the more we experience, the stronger we grow. The paradox of suffering is that, through difficulties, we gain the armor of psychological residue. Every terrible experience prepares us for the next until we—and our future generations—are unshakable.

PART THREE

CONCRETE BARRIERS

CHAPTER 8

NAVIGATING THE CONCRETE BARRIERS

WHEN I WAS in the military, I was demoted in rank.

Having joined as a young man, I suddenly found myself with the newfound independence of adulthood. And, in the military, the drinking culture is strong.

What's the harm, I thought, of knocking back a drink or five after a hard day's work?

My white friend thought the same, and, before I knew it, we were in trouble for underage drinking. We'd entered the military at the same time and were moving up in rank together. Except when we got caught drinking, he got a slap on the wrist. I got demoted.

This left me permanently behind him, even though we'd done exactly the same things—good and bad—throughout our careers.

Of course, I was furious.

I could've fallen apart. I could've rebelled, fighting back until I was discharged. I could've collapsed into myself, giving in to anger and anxiety. I could've stopped trying, throwing my hands up and waiting for the end of my enlistment.

Maybe those things would have been justified. But they would have only hurt me. The system that punished me differently because

I'm African American would not have cared. None of those actions would have corrected the racism I'd experienced.

So instead, I set my jaw and pushed on with my career. I'd joined the military at twenty years old because I wanted to experience the entire United States. I wanted to see the world.

I wasn't about to let an unfair, discriminatory decision take that away from me.

Rather than quitting or lashing out, I took note of what I'd experienced. Whether it was fair or not, treatment and consequences for me as a Black man would be harsher than for my white counterparts. I realized I needed to be aware of the rules of the system—next time, I'd see it coming.

In the following years, I got to see how different cultures live. I learned how they understood the meaning of life. Through conversations with diverse people, I discovered new things about my own culture. Sometimes, I felt proud—I was part of the US Military, which was something bigger than myself. Other times, people asked me things like, "why is your country so racist?" or "how can you live in America?" They'd ask me how it felt to be a Black guy in a racist country. Our American ideology isn't perfect, and that was never clearer than when I realized that every other country viewed mine as racist.

I grew a lot from those conversations—my worldview broadened, and I began to see things differently. I set my mind to rise through the ranks. As an African American, I'd experienced a lot of microaggressions and macroaggressions in my life. But I'd also developed a no-fail mentality. I had an internal drive to do better than everybody else, because I had to, regardless of my circumstances.

My mom gave me that. A fierce black queen on a chess board with odds aggressively stacked against her, my mom had to find ways to push through her circumstances. I decided I would, too.

But as I rose through the ranks, the whole board became clearer. I could see beyond my own moves. Traveling around the world gave me a perspective I hadn't had before. Like zooming out on a camera, I was able to see the rules of the game much more clearly. Suddenly, I found myself in the political ranks of the military, contributing to the rules of a game I knew was stacked against me.

When we're so close to racism, it can feel like a constant battle. The moment we swat away one microaggression, another comes along—we can barely keep up in our day-to-day lives, let alone look to the future.

But when I traveled away from the United States, I was finally able to see our country's racism for what it was—a series of concrete barriers to navigate.

This is why looking at the big picture is so important. Like chess players, we have to look at the whole board and anticipate the moves that will come three or four or more turns later. That's the only way to out-maneuver an opponent.

We can use our resiliency to navigate concrete barriers in exactly the same way—and we can use those barriers to strengthen ourselves even more.

Imagine America's racism as a system—a game—with rules, strategies, and predictable patterns. To return to our chess metaphor, think of African Americans as the black pieces and white America as the white pieces. As we discussed a few chapters ago, the white player moves first. It's easy for the black player to fall immediately into defensive mode.

But, of course, that's a fatal mistake in the game of chess—and in life. Instead, we need to remind ourselves to play offense throughout the game. We make our moves based not only on rules and laws, but also on our lives. With each move, we bring in our own belief system and experiences. Some of us prefer to make moves on the right-hand side of the board. Others might like to start off to the left.

Regardless of how a player prefers to start, there's one thing all good players have in common: we're never in a hurry. Hurry is uncontrolled. It's messy.

If we want to win in chess, we have to wait for a moment that we can exploit in our favor.

Winning takes patience.

Our ancestors knew that. They took their time, and when they saw an opening, they seized it.

It can be very difficult to wait for that perfect opportunity—it can feel passive. But because our ancestors did it before us, we can do it, too. Concrete barriers—rules and laws designed to keep us behind and defensive—are just like any other challenge. We can reframe them with optimism, thinking of them as opportunities to grow through suffering.

But, to do that, we have to remember our epigenetic strength and practice cognitive restructuring. We must avoid anxiety and recklessness. That way, we can keep our minds on offense—waiting for that perfect moment—rather than ruminating on what just happened or how we messed up.

Sometimes we make a wrong move in chess. We slide right when we should have jumped left. This is just the same in life—our decisions aren't always perfect. But as long as we have optimism, we can stay cool and collected and look at ways to use that wrong move in our favor.

And just as I looked to my mom for inspiration, we can all look to our ancestors for strength. We know how to play the game—we've seen them do it. Sometimes it just takes a little reminder that generations of struggle gave us even more than resiliency.

They also gave us ingenuity.

CONCRETE BARRIERS AND MULTI-GENERATIONAL INGENUITY

We gain ingenuity not only from our own experiences—zooming out as we learn more about the world—but also from watching other African Americans navigate it. Because our friends, family, and community members are also encoded with transgenerational resiliency, observing others is our opportunity to see that optimistic DNA in action.

This is what we mean when we talk about multi-generational

ingenuity—our ability to anticipate concrete barriers because we've seen others navigate them before us. Our ancestors who fought for Civil Rights in the 1950s and 1960s had seen their parents and grandparents build strategies to survive Jim Crow. They'd built those strategies from seeing their own parents and grandparents navigate slavery. And today, four hundred years from the time the first enslaved Africans set foot on American soil, we're still watching previous generations and learning from their strategies—those tactics have been so refined that they are almost second nature to us.

This was never clearer than in the police murder of Philando Castile.

In the horrifying video that circulated in the summer of 2016, a white police officer shot Castile less than one minute from the time he'd pulled the car over. Millions of viewers watched the Facebook live video, recorded by his girlfriend Diamond Reynolds, and saw the marked difference between the police officer's mental state and the mental state of the African American man, woman, and child in the car that day. At one point, Reynolds narrates the interaction, her boyfriend dying in the seat next to her. The police officer's voice rises to a fever pitch of anxiety as he shouts and pleads with her, unhinged in his reaction to his own violent behavior.

Reynolds, on the other hand, remains so collected that she is able to correct the officer as he rants about the sequence of events, her voice calm and almost soothing. An incredibly strong Black woman, Reynolds draws upon a resiliency embedded in her DNA by generations before her.

That's not all I see when I watch that terrible video—I also see an African American woman's ingenuity. Having watched other Black women before her, she knows that the stereotype of the "angry Black woman" would only be used against her. She knows in her bones that remaining calm is the only way to protect her own life and the life of her daughter. So, she does. That's the defensive black queen.

But she's also, quietly and strategically, playing offense. By pulling out her phone—slowly and with total control—and seamlessly starting a Facebook live video, she recruited the entire nation in support of her boyfriend. She saw a hole in the system, one that was first opened twenty-five years earlier when George Holliday used his Handycam to film Rodney King's beating at the hands of LA police.

While the white police officer panicked outside the passenger window of Philando Castile's car, Diamond Reynolds played both defense and offense. As African American women—Black queens—always do, she both protected herself *and* advocated for the people she loved.

Police violence against African Americans has existed as long as police have existed. That's why generations of African Americans have had "the talk" with their children, preparing them for the best odds of survival if confronted with an officer like the one who killed Castile. Most of us have also seen our parents interact with police or someone else in a threatening position of power.

That means we grew up seeing the concrete barriers. Before we even knew what we were experiencing, we'd gotten an aerial view of the chess board. We saw the rules, and in turn, the strategies to get around them.

This is how multi-generational ingenuity is created—it's built up, like epigenetic strength—through generations of refinement and reinforcement.

And it shows not just in life-or-death situations like this one. From the time when we are very young, we witness African American ingenuity in all kinds of ways. We learn that we can't yell and make a scene in a public place. If we fly in an airplane or eat at a restaurant, we can't scream at the servers. We can't constantly ask to speak to the manager. It might be dangerous, and it wouldn't be effective.

Instead, we learn to find creative ways to exploit the system—to find our way around concrete barriers. Maybe I can't demand to speak to the manager, but I can go online and write a review. I can use social media to contact the corporate office and report my issue there. Unfair as it may be, those strategies allow me to conceal my race or find someone who won't treat me differently because of it.

That's optimism. That's seeing a concrete barrier not as a reason to quit, but as a reason to think more creatively. It's zooming out, so we can see the size and scope of the concrete barrier—and, as it turns out, there's usually a way to navigate around it, even when it seems impossible.

If we can see the big picture, we can find a way to use our transgenerational resiliency to chart a course around the barriers and accomplish everything we set out to do.

CHARTING HER OWN COURSE: BESSIE COLEMAN

Bessie Coleman was the first African American woman to earn an international pilot's license. Like most historic firsts, doing so wasn't easy. Born in 1892 in Atlanta, Texas, Coleman and her twelve siblings watched their parents struggle for every penny. Her mother worked as a maid, and her father, who had both Native American and Black ancestry, was a sharecropper. The work was hard, and the children were often called upon to help.

Coleman knew the aches and scratches of picking cotton for hours on end.

She tried to attend college, hoping to build a better life for herself. However, unable to afford tuition, she dropped out after only a semester. She then moved to Chicago to attend beauty school. While she was there, her brother returned from France, where he'd served in World War I.

His stories gave her an idea.

While she'd dreamed of flying, none of America's pilot training programs accepted African Americans—and they didn't accept women, either.

Coleman could have given up right then. At the turn of the twentieth century, the United States was an inhospitable place for a woman with both Black and Native American blood. But she refused. Growing up in Texas, she'd seen generations of African Americans navigate difficult times, and she set out to find a way around the barriers.

Programs in Europe had started accepting women, but there was one big problem—Coleman had never lived outside the United States. She knew nothing about European culture or languages.

So, she learned.

Determined to succeed, Coleman took French classes at night, learning enough of the language to complete her application. She scraped and saved for the money to move overseas and, eventually, she had it.

In 1921, she completed a program at the Cauldron Brothers School of Aviation and earned her international pilot's license.

It's difficult to think of a more ingenious way to navigate around the system. But ingenuity didn't make it easy. She still had to hold together her mental toughness. She had to be incredibly patient as she learned a new language and saved money for her move. And she had to persist, even when so many others would have given up.

That kind of resiliency was in her blood, whether she knew it or not.

By the mid-1920s, Coleman was famous for her daring feats of flight. She'd specialized in stunt flying and gathered crowds not only as the first African American woman to fly in public—but as one of the most talented pilots of any race or gender.

And it soon became clear that she'd found another way to exploit the holes in the system. When she wasn't busy touring with her stunt show, she gave flying lessons, using her skills to encourage other African American women pilots.

Coleman wasn't content just to be the first. She wanted to make sure she wasn't the last.

As she grew more and more famous, she used that recognition as leverage, refusing to perform for segregated audiences. While she couldn't change the laws of the land, she saw a way she could improve circumstances for future generations of African Americans —she could help change the culture.

And she did. Persisting through countless difficulties, including a plane crash that left her with multiple injuries, she held strong to her vision of the future. She developed increasingly dangerous tricks, earning enough money to purchase her own plane, and showing the world that African American women weren't just as good as white men—they could be even better.

For her next trick, she promised, she would open an aviation school exclusively for African Americans.

Unfortunately, she wouldn't live to see her dream come true.

During a rehearsal for an air show, she was thrown from her plane and died tragically, at only thirty-four years old.

But even in her short life, Coleman had proven that anything was possible with patience, resiliency, and ingenuity. She perfectly demonstrated the art of playing both offense and defense, as she worked first alongside her mother and later in a nail salon, saving up until she saw an opening to achieve her dreams.

I'm sure there were days when she wanted to quit. I'm sure there were days she worried about discrimination—or worse. But she held strong, resisting the anxiety loop and holding herself steady until she achieved her dreams—then she dreamed some more.

And, because Coleman succeeded so publicly, her achievement spreading faster and farther from the sheer spectacle of her work, the nation knew that African American women could be pilots. In the end, she not only navigated the concrete barriers—she smashed through them, destroying them forever.

Coleman not only benefited from the optimism and resiliency of her own ancestors—she passed it on. Although she never had children of her own, African American girls across the country saw her. Her ingenuity had extended generations before her, and, through her courage and determination, it extended far into future generations.

THE RULES OF THE GAME

As African Americans, we are surrounded by concrete barriers. We face everything from racial violence to microaggressions. We could just give up and accept the hand we've been dealt. But generations of ancestors worked hard to create strength, resiliency, and optimism in our DNA.

They also passed on their ingenuity. By watching other African Americans navigate the concrete barriers around us, we've learned ways to game the system. We can zoom out and observe the rules and laws of the chess board in front of us. Forced to play both defense *and* offense, we have the capacity to remain calm in the face of violence and discrimination, to wait patiently for an opening to exploit the rules.

This was precisely what Bessie Coleman did. By learning French and moving to Europe, she found a way to move around the concrete barriers. And through her actions, she paved the way for others.

To do so, she had to control her anxiety.

The following chapter will explore why cognitive restructuring and breaking the anxiety loop are crucial not only for our own survival, but also to make the world better for future generations of African Americans.

CHAPTER 9
HOW ANXIETY BLOCKS SOCIAL CHANGE

A FEW YEARS AGO, I had a conversation with a friend that dramatically reshaped how I see the world. We hadn't seen each other in a while, and he'd invited me out to grab a beer after work. As we talked about our lives, I noticed that the themes of optimism and persistence kept coming up.

He'd been saving up to purchase an investment home at the time —he planned to fix up a little house and rent it to a family.

But his own family didn't think he could do it. They thought it would be too much work, too much money, and too much trouble to find stable renters.

He laughed when he told me. "It's great that they said that, honestly," he said. "Because it just makes me want to do it more!"

"Exactly," I chuckled. "When someone says, 'you can't do that,' I'm like, 'yes, I can, you jerk.'"

We laughed at that and took a few more swigs of beer.

Then he told me something I carry with me today.

"Have you ever heard of the Kalahari tribe?" he asked. "Or sometimes they're called the 'Bushmen'?"

"I've heard of them, sure," I replied. "What about them?" "They do this thing called 'persistence hunting.' Basically, they just run after wild animals."

I looked at him inquisitively. "They just run?"

"They just run!" he laughed. "But they always catch their prey because they refuse to give up. Eventually, the animal gets tired." He nodded and sipped his beer. "They're the best long-distance runners in the world. They almost always catch the animal."

I've thought about that anecdote a lot since then. To me, it says a lot about the relationship between optimism and persistence. It takes a lot of optimism to keep running, hour after hour, in the heat of the sun, just trusting that you'll outlast a wild animal. Without that optimism, it would be easy to give up—after all, what's the point of running if you don't think you'll ever catch your next meal?

Some days, I'm sure, it's incredibly difficult for them to keep moving. They must fantasize about retreating into the shade to rest. At times, the wilderness shadows must play tricks on them, giving the appearance of an animal right around the corner when the kudu they're chasing is actually far ahead in the distance.

But if they give up, their families would go hungry. And then their families would give up, too. Morale would tank. With nothing to eat and no way to get food, they might give in to their lack of hope.

Most of us would give up well before we caught a wild animal. Because what the Bushmen have isn't just optimism—it's generational optimism. From the time they're very young, they train for the hunt, building up their endurance over hours, weeks, months, and years until they're unstoppable. And, because their ancestors could do it, they know they can do it too. So they keep training, persistent in the face of certain failure, until that failure isn't so certain anymore. They keep training until they get what they need. The Kalahari tribe can teach us a lot about how to handle adversity. By focusing our minds on optimism—resiliency—we can persist through anything. That's not easy, not by a long shot. When our brains sense danger and uncertainty, they often turn to the anxiety loop, repeating the negative over and over.

As we've discussed in previous chapters, this is an effect of the sympathetic nervous system—the part of the brain responsible for what we often call "fight or flight" mode. The sympathetic nervous system can pop up to undermine our efforts at work, in our relationships, or even in our leisure time.

But what we can learn from persistence hunting—as well as other adversarial events—is that the sympathetic nervous system can also cause much larger problems. It can undermine our very existence and prevent us from being able to navigate the concrete barriers that pop up in our everyday lives.

The only way to continue to fight for social change is to get our anxiety in check—and the only way to do that is by reigning in our sympathetic nervous systems.

THE SYMPATHETIC AND PARASYMPATHETIC NERVOUS SYSTEM

Nothing triggers the sympathetic nervous system like a concrete barrier. From anxious, violent police officers to teachers that would rather see us kicked out of school than wearing a durag, each of these concrete barriers is a literal threat to our continued existence. Whether physical, emotional, social, or psychological, they trigger our brains to take action to sustain our lives.

This fight-or-flight response is a neurological feature, leftover from when our very early ancestors had to battle the harshest elements of nature to survive. In other words, it helps us protect ourselves.

When the fight-or-flight response, or the sympathetic nervous system, is activated, it releases a hormone called adrenaline. Adrenaline increases our heart rate and makes us breathe faster. It also gives us a burst of energy so we can either fight or flee from the threat.

When our very early ancestors came face to face with a hungry wolf, that adrenaline was their only chance to survive. It energized them to run away, climb a tree, or, if they were feeling lucky, kill the wolf.

Most of us don't encounter wolves in our everyday lives. But we do face concrete barriers. And adrenaline can have a very different effect on us when we're faced with racism.

Like most African Americans, I learned this young.

My junior high school didn't allow students to wear durags. This policy is, of course, deeply racist. Durags have been worn by Black people for centuries, and banning them sends the message that Black culture is not valued or welcome in schools. It also creates an environment where African American students feel ostracized and isolated. Banning durags is a form of racial discrimination—a concrete barrier worth breaking down.

But that's not why I continued to wear a durag to school even after I was told not to. I continued to wear a durag because, like most thirteen-year-olds, I wanted to look my best. Unfortunately, I had ingrown hairs on the back of my neck. I wore it to cover them.

I remember the first time a teacher approached me about it, a forty-year-old man threatening a kid about their clothing.

"I'm not taking it off," I told him, not even hesitating after he told me to remove my durag.

"Then you're going to sit in detention and think about why you can't follow school policy."

"What?!" I protested. Now my adrenaline was really firing—this white man had set off my temper, and my sympathetic nervous system was telling me to fight. I pointed to a white kid a few desks over. "But Nick gets to wear his cowboy hat?! How is that fair?!" I leaned back in my seat and crossed my arms, fuming.

"You've got a half hour now. Wanna make it an hour?"

"No," I grumbled. I wanted to say more. I wanted to tell him he was racist. I wanted to tell him how regressive the stupid policy was. But I was an African American kid, pitted against not only an adult teacher, but an entire white-centered school system. There wasn't much I could do.

That didn't stop the adrenaline from flowing. That first day, I just sat in detention and stewed in my anger. The punishment was totally unfair and clearly biased. Although I didn't know how to describe it at the time, I walked home that day with my sympathetic nervous system on fire.

Fortunately, I wasn't just angry—I was also calculating.

The next day, I wore my durag, just like I had the day before. The teacher assigned me detention, just like the day before, but I kept my cool.

And then, I spent detention doing my homework.

When my friends teased me, calling me an "Uncle Tom" and criticizing me for "just shutting up when the white guy told me to do something," I reminded them that my homework was done. They had to finish their math problems that night. I enjoyed a relaxing evening of listening to music in my room.

I didn't realize what I was doing at the time, but by listening to music, I was engaging my parasympathetic nervous system.

The parasympathetic nervous system is the opposite of the sympathetic nervous system. It's often referred to as the rest-and-digest or feed-and-breed response because it helps us do just that: rest, eat, and enjoy a romantic evening with our partners.

When the parasympathetic nervous system is activated, it slows our heart rate and makes us breathe more slowly. It also increases blood flow to our digestive system so we can properly break down and absorb our food. In short, the parasympathetic nervous system helps us relax, while the sympathetic nervous system helps us prepare for action.

The parasympathetic nervous system is important in evolution because it helps us relax and reduce anxiety. This allows us to better handle stress and survive in challenging situations.

The parasympathetic nervous system developed in early humans as a way to help them cope with the challenges of survival. Over time, it has become an essential part of our stress-management arsenal.

Learning how to control our parasympathetic nervous system can be a valuable tool in managing anxiety and stress. By becoming more aware of our anxiety triggers and learning relaxation techniques, we can help keep our nervous system functioning properly.

Any relaxation technique can help us strengthen our parasympathetic nervous system, so you've probably been doing it your entire life without realizing it. Even as a high school student making mix tapes on my boombox, I was training my body to relax and rest, setting me up to thoughtfully and strategically navigate the concrete barriers that came my way.

Eventually, I trained myself to react to that teacher with a calm resolution. He thought he was punishing me, but I was using his anger to my advantage. And it all felt even better because I kept my cool and persisted in pursuing my own goals, eventually breaking down the concrete barrier that attempted to keep me from finishing high school. But imagine the alternative. If I had let that teacher get to me, I might have kept fighting, but I doubt I would have changed anything. As long as my fight-or-flight response was triggered, I would have only escalated the situation, making things worse for myself and changing very little about the concrete barriers that were in my way.

Because the harsh truth is that our sympathetic nervous systems will never create change. That fight-or-flight response can have a useful function when we're approached by a wolf or if we need to flee from any modern imminent danger. But it has no function in the slow, steady progress of social change.

To change the world—to really make a lasting difference—we have to march forward with the calm, steady resolve that can only come from our parasympathetic nervous system.

And that was exactly what protesters did on March 7, 1965.

MARCHING FORWARD INTO ADVERSITY

On that sunny afternoon, Martin Luther King, Jr. led a group of people from Selma to Montgomery, Alabama. Before that day,

African Americans were not guaranteed the right to vote, and King believed that a major demonstration was needed to ensure that the entire country saw the struggles that Black people faced.

Many famous people attended the march including Coretta Scott King, Ralph Abernathy, and Amelia Boynton. More than 25,000 people gathered to start the march, but only 2,000 made it all the way to Montgomery.

The group was attacked by state troopers on the Edmund Pettus Bridge, and this event became known as "Bloody Sunday." The troopers used tear gas and clubs to beat the protesters, and seventeen people were hospitalized. This event led to more outrage and more people became involved in the Civil Rights Movement.

The voting rights act was introduced in Congress that very day, and it was signed into law five months later, no doubt in part because of the protesters' efforts.

In retrospect, the action seems like a clear victory. But if we put ourselves in the position of those protesters, the picture becomes much more complex.

For the protesters who made it to the end of the march, they must have been terrified to see the state troopers waiting for them. For many of them, this must have been one of the scariest moments of their lives. And yet, heart pounding and palms sweaty, many of them continued forward, crossing over fifty miles of terrain.

Whether they knew it or not, they had transgenerational resiliency. They borrowed strength, courage, and determination from their ancestors before them, and used them to see the course, walking tall and strong even in the threat of extreme violence.

They must have had something else, too, though. Some of the protesters didn't make it to the end. Overcome by fear or exhaustion, they dropped from the line and went home—it was an understandable path, particularly in the face of miles and miles of walking.

But imagine if they had all given up. Imagine if they had given into the anxiety that coursed through their bodies—imagine if they had chosen "flight." At this crucial moment in Civil Rights history, their persistence was rewarded not only with the Voting Rights Act, but also with the continuation of advocacy. It was by no means guaranteed—as with all points in history, there was a strong white backlash to King's actions, as evidenced by the violent response of the Alabama state troopers. If they had stopped their march and retreated as the troopers—and their own sympathetic nervous systems—instructed them, much of their progress might have been undone.

So how did they persist in the face of this extreme threat?

They must have allowed the determination of their ancestors to speak not to their fight-or-flight center, but to their parasympathetic nervous system. They knew they couldn't give into anxiety and fear. If they wanted to move forward, even after the exhaustion of miles—and years—of striving for voting rights, they must have known that they had to stay calm, cool, and collected. They had to show America —including fellow African Americans, white people, and those of other races—that they were serious, thoughtful change-makers. And the only way they could do that is by tamping down their anxiety and staying the course.

The Pettus bridge marchers knew that anxiety blocks social change. As long as we allow ourselves to fall into the anxiety loop, focusing on the things we can't change and the dangers that await us if we try, we will never be able to move forward toward true equality.

Fortunately, like those who walked the Pettus bridge, we have the strength of our ancestors to carry us forward.

But we must also do our part, strengthening our parasympathetic nervous systems to make ourselves stronger and more resilient in the face of the concrete barriers we encounter every single day.

EXERCISE: PRACTICING MINDFULNESS

There are many ways to train your parasympathetic nervous system. Listening to music, spending time in nature, doing yoga, or practicing muscle relaxation can all teach our brains to access the relax-and-digest function more easily. But the most targeted approach is to practice mindfulness.

In this exercise, we'll practice basic mindfulness techniques. Some people find mindfulness intimidating. But mindfulness is simply paying attention to the present moment, without judgment.

Prepare

Choose a comfortable spot to sit or lie down. You can close your eyes if you'd like, but it's not necessary.

Place your hand on your stomach and breathe deeply, directing your breath deep into your belly. While sometimes our breathing can get shallow, making our chest move up and down, when you perform mindfulness, try to keep the majority of the movement on your stomach—make your belly pop out like Santa Claus, and keep your hand on your stomach so you can feel the movement.

Breathe

Inhale, feeling your hand move outward with the breath, then exhale slowly. Inhale again, thinking of your belly as a balloon. Inflate the balloon, then gently push the air back out. This type of breathing fills up the bottom of your lungs near your diaphragm. By shifting your breath down into your belly, you relieve pressure on your heart caused by shallow breathing and consequently lower your heart rate. This type of deep breathing also helps you to relax your shoulders, since your chest isn't struggling to contain our airflow.

Observe

Continue to breathe deeply through your belly, in and out, in and out, and simply focus on your body. You might feel an ache in your shoulders, your breath might hitch a little in your chest, or you might find your brain cycling through anxiety. Acknowledge those sensations, then let them float out of your mind, returning your focus back to the breath.

As you continue breathing, you'll begin to feel a physiological response. Just as you do when you enter the anxiety loop, you will notice your body changing—but in this case, you'll notice a restful change.

As you continue your exercise, take note of that change. That's all mindfulness is—noticing how your body is responding to its environment. Feel your body relaxing, and keep breathing into that relaxation.

Practice

At first, even five minutes will feel like an eternity. We aren't used to sitting quietly and focusing on our bodies. So, start small. Practice your breathing for just two or three minutes at first. Over time, once you feel more comfortable with mindfulness, you can increase the amount of time to five minutes, then six, then seven. The purpose is simply to slow down and remind your body that you are safe, strong, and resilient. There is no need for fight-or-flight. Everything you want to achieve can be done with steady, thoughtful actions —and they all require rest.

Break the Anxiety Loop

Mindfulness helps us to harness our parasympathetic nervous system, ensuring that we can build on the resiliency we've inherited from our ancestors. This is crucial, since calm, steady growth is the only way we can effectively create social change—not only navigating the concrete barriers we face, but tearing them down for future generations, just as our ancestors did for us.

In the next chapter, we'll take this approach a step further, considering how we can use our parasympathetic nervous system to play the proverbial "long game," and ensure that we stick around to fight for as long as it takes.

CHAPTER 10
ACCEPT, FORGIVE, WIN

A COUPLE OF YEARS AGO, my kids discovered *The Lion King*. I loved that movie when I was growing up, so I didn't mind at first. Then we watched it again. And again. And again. And, after what felt like hundreds of rewatches, I started to tune out the happy music and the devastating, heartbreaking moments.

I started to think about the meaning of the story for African American transgenerational resiliency. Based on African history, the story has a lot to tell us about how we understand our place in the world in relation to others. It reveals the dangers of acting impulsively and delves into the psychological struggles of fear, grief, and guilt.

But most notably, it teaches us about anger.

The story of *The Lion King* is really the story of three types of rulers. There's Mufasa, the strong, muscular king with a flowing mane. Simba, his son, is just a cub when the film opens. He grows up curious and tender, but only through extreme hardships and an eventual redemption story. And, finally, there's Scar. Mufasa's brother, Scar feels entitled to the throne and angry that his brother became King of Pride Rock. At some point in the movie, each of the rulers displays righteous anger—they've encountered something unfair or disappointing, and it quite understandably makes them mad.

Mufasa's anger is the most visually striking. Never flustered or uncontrolled, Mufasa feels angry at his son for running away. And he's quite reasonably angry when his brother attempts to steal his position. But Mufasa always handles his anger in productive ways. Calm and rational, his anger sparks ideas—it makes him think about how he can best solve the problem he's facing. He can go after Simba, retrieve him, and have a beautiful father-son moment, explaining the importance of listening and disciplining Simba for his dangerous behavior. Even attempting to reason with his horrible brother, Scar, Mufasa turns his anger into communication, using it to fix the problems he encounters.

Mufasa seems to realize, at least intuitively, that anger is a healthy, normal emotion. A natural feeling in our bodies, anger shouldn't be suppressed or ignored—it simply must be processed.

The healthy kind of anger, Mufasa anger is about clear, level-headed thinking and measured communication.

Simba anger is very different. Although the movie follows Simba as he grows from cub to king, it is during Simba's childhood that we most clearly see his anger. Simba is angry that his father died. If you've lost a parent or other family member, you can probably relate to his feeling—it's natural to feel angry when we experience extreme loss. We want someone to blame. And when there is no one to blame, we often blame ourselves—just as Simba did.

Just like Simba, we can find ourselves isolated and alone. Simba refused to deal with his anger at all. Instead, he pushed it to the side, running away and avoiding the pain.

This approach to anger can be incredibly damaging to our emotional and mental health. Not only is it about avoiding a natural emotion in our bodies—it also means ignoring who we are.

When Mufasa dies, Simba's anger sends him into the wasteland. He pushes his anger down hard, repressing it in himself, and instead of returning to the pride to talk about what happened, he scrounges in the dirt for bugs to eat. But lions aren't supposed to eat bugs. Lions eat meat.

By repressing and avoiding his anger, Simba found himself behaving more like a bird or a reptile than a lion. In other words, this type of anger robbed Simba of his true identity. Suppressed anger also robs us of our whole selves.

Finally, there's Scar anger. Scar anger is pure chaos. We hope not to relate to this type of anger—the anger that makes us want to destroy everyone and everything—but most of us have felt it at some point in our lives.

While Scar anger might look different from Simba anger, they share some commonalities. Both are about avoiding our true emotions. Both cause us to retreat into ourselves, and we refuse to communicate our feelings to others. And both are unhealthy and, ultimately, self-destructive.

These three angers—Mufasa anger, Simba anger, and Scar anger—are all natural responses to disappointment. When we encounter concrete barriers in our daily lives, we may experience any one of these types of anger. We might even cycle through all three.

Believe it or not, that's a good thing.

Anger protects us. It protects our values, our beliefs, our feelings, and our identities. In fact, this is the very reason we get angry in the first place—something or someone is trying to break through our deepest, most intimately held beliefs. Our bodies respond by sending that jolt of anger through us.

Our job is to figure out why we're angry. By doing so, we can channel Mufasa, using our anger in healthy ways and avoiding the self-destructive tendencies of Simba and Scar. But, of course, it's not always so simple—and it's never easy.

THE MEANING OF ANGER

The anger we feel at concrete barriers is righteous and real.

We shouldn't have to fear for our lives at simple traffic stops. Our kids shouldn't be harassed in school because of their hairstyles. And our ancestors shouldn't have had to endure firehoses and dogs when they advocated for fair treatment—they shouldn't have had to advocate in the first place.

It's reasonable to feel angry about these things.

Unfortunately, anger does little to break down concrete barriers. We can channel our anger into productive actions—strategies that make the world more equitable—but doing so requires much more than emotion. To use anger productively, we have to tap into our resiliency and consider the most practical ways to move forward.

This is especially important in our day-to-day lives, where concrete barriers can sometimes be difficult to recognize. Often, those barriers present themselves in ways that make them seem personal, disguising society's racist patterns.

I was working with a client recently whose father had been absent for most of her life. Rayna had a lot of anger for her father, and most of it wasn't serving her well. She talked a lot about disappointments she'd experienced as a child. Often, her father would forget to pick her up from school. Embarrassed, she would wait outside the building as long as she could. She often gave up and went back inside to call her mother. Sometimes she had to walk home, disappointed and hurt that her father didn't care enough to show up when he was supposed to. The anger she'd felt then—anger that still reemerged from time to time—was Scar anger. Chaotic and difficult to explain, rage filled her chest when she remembered those childhood moments.

Then, when Rayna was a teenager, her father went to prison for drug possession. Police had raided his apartment in the middle of the night and found marijuana and some prescription drugs he'd bought from a friend. As a young adult, Rayna hadn't cared about the reasons. She only knew that he was gone from her life—and he never returned. When he called, she refused to accept the charges, and she never went to visit him. He was just gone.

As a defense mechanism, she shut out the anger, declaring their relationship over. She still cared about him—although she insisted that she didn't—but she couldn't face the anger. Like Simba, she ran away from the pain.

After weeks of talking through the ways her father had disappointed her over the years, I finally stopped her.

"What's a *positive* quality about your dad?" I asked.

She stared at me. "A positive quality?"

I nodded.

After a few seconds, she said, "I guess...I always thought he was really funny."

"Okay," I continued. "What do you mean?"

"When he would take me to the park, he would play right along with me." She smiled to herself. "I remember once he got on the little rocking animal things at the park. All the kids were laughing, he looked so funny."

I let her reflect for a moment.

"You know, now that I think about it," she continued. "He was kind of like a kid."

"Do you think maybe he didn't know how to be a dad?"

"One hundred percent," she said confidently.

"What do you think he went through as he was trying to raise you?"

She crossed her arms. "He didn't try to raise me!"

"Are you sure?" I asked.

She nodded. "I guess I don't really know. I remember that my mom said it wasn't fair when he went to prison. She always called it a 'bullshit drug charge.'"

The longer we talked, the more Rayna softened. It wasn't that her father had been perfect—far from it. But Rayna had been so focused on her own anger that it prevented her from seeing the concrete barriers her father had faced. He hadn't been ready to be a father, she realized, and once he wound up in prison, he couldn't do much to improve.

By considering the meaning of her anger and the ways it was hurting her, she was able to make those emotions more productive.

She didn't immediately drive to the prison to reunite with her father —her pain was too deep for that, at least at the moment. But she finally allowed herself to feel the natural, rational anger that had built up for most of her life. By doing that, she was able to recognize her own strength—she finally realized who she was and where she came from.

Earlier in this book, you completed similar exercises, finding the resiliency in your ancestors and identifying some of the barriers they faced. But that alone isn't always enough to channel our anger from avoidance and chaos into action and communication.

The only way to achieve that goal is to reshape our anger. By considering the role of acceptance and forgiveness, we can embrace our anger as a natural tool in our journey of transgenerational resiliency.

THE DIFFERENCE BETWEEN ACCEPTANCE AND FORGIVENESS

As someone who tended toward avoidance, Rayna had a long road ahead of her. She needed to face what she'd experienced and process her anger—and she had to learn to accept it. Many of us fight similar battles in our own lives, particularly when it comes to concrete barriers. It can be easier to approach everyday microaggressions through avoidance. And when we experience discrimination, it can cause a chaotic type of anger that takes our emotions hostage, flooding our brains with adrenaline and short-circuiting our ability to think calmly and clearly.

When we experience these things, acceptance can seem counterproductive—even wrong. But acceptance can be a useful tool to honor our ancestors, build resiliency for future generations, and live our best lives now.

Forgiveness, on the other hand, serves a very different function.

Let's begin by defining acceptance and forgiveness.

Acceptance is an alternative to avoidance. To accept, we must be aware of the historical, social, and environmental challenges of being

Black in America. Acceptance doesn't mean ignoring history or our own experiences. It simply means understanding those factors intellectually—without prescribing a particular emotion to them.

This is easier said than done. Experiencing microaggressions in our everyday life can stir up intense anger, frustration, embarrassment, and stress. But by accepting what happened, we choose to acknowledge the harm that was done to us without dwelling on it. We don't allow ourselves to fall into the anxiety loop because we don't attach negative emotions to the event.

Acceptance simply means realizing that our experiences are part of a long pattern in this country. Although there have always been emotional responses to the horrors of racism in the US, those emotions alone have never changed anything—because emotions aren't the same as actions.

When we approach things this way, it becomes clear that there is very little value in an overly emotional response. Life isn't fair, and no amount of anger will change that—all we can do is choose how we respond.

When we accept our experiences of discrimination, we don't excuse them. But we don't try to change them either, at least not in the moment. In the moment of acceptance, we realize that we must come to terms with both who and where we are, realizing that lashing out, avoiding, or taking on chaotic anger can cause lasting psychological harm.

Acceptance doesn't mean giving up. But if we don't accept things for what they are now, we'll never be able to progress forward to the *future*. We'll never make things better.

As African Americans, we must accept who we are in the United States. Our enslaved ancestors built this country. We've always been mothers, brothers, sisters, fathers, spiritual figures, doctors, lawyers, lovers, and fighters, but we haven't always been acknowledged that way. That's our history. Those are our families.

To deny that is to deny who we are.

This is why acceptance is different from forgiveness.

Forgiveness goes beyond acceptance—it's about acknowledging that someone has wronged you but choosing not to let that wrong harm the relationship. When we forgive someone, we communicate that we understand the harm they've done to us, but that we choose not to dwell on it. Dwelling on the ways others have harmed us can leave us unhappy and isolated, and it usually destroys our relationship with the person.

We forgive when we want to maintain the ties—when we want to acknowledge that a harm was done, but when we trust that the person didn't intend that harm, and that they won't repeat it in the future. Forgiveness doesn't mean forgetting. It simply means prioritizing the relationship over the wrong.

It's crucially important that we accept the history of racism in the US. Without acknowledging what our ancestors endured—the experiences that allowed them to strengthen their DNA and give us the gift of transgenerational resiliency—we can't really know who we are.

We have to accept America's history of racism. But we don't have to forgive.

Acceptance changes both our internal self-talk and our external action and behaviors. To have transgenerational resiliency is to accept that events occurred—to look those painful experiences, memories, and history lessons square in the eye without flinching. There can be no avoidance or disconnection.

By accepting things for what they are—with our present families and our past ancestors in mind—we can finally navigate concrete barriers effectively. This can alleviate the stress, anxiety, and poor performance that comes with avoidance because it allows us to approach things with a cool head and a strategic eye. In other words, it makes us more resilient.

Acceptance isn't just about acknowledging our negative experiences. It's also about accepting our own strength. It's about realizing that pain is inevitable, but suffering is not.

There is no better way to prepare ourselves for the concrete barriers that lie ahead.

There is no other way to win.

CONCRETE BARRIERS: KEY POINTS

In this section, we've applied transgenerational resiliency to the concrete barriers of racism in America. While these barriers have always been in place, it's crucial that we approach them with a spirit of strength and optimism, rather than anxiety and anger.

The transgenerational resiliency approach to concrete barriers includes the following key points.

Generational Ingenuity

Our ancestors left us more than resiliency—they also passed down generations of ingenuity. African Americans have always faced concrete barriers, and while sometimes we can work together to knock them down, we can also find creative ways to navigate around them. By figuring out the rules of the game, no matter how unfair, we can chart our own course. In that way, we break new ground—just like Bessie Coleman—by outsmarting white supremacy.

The Sympathetic and Parasympathetic Nervous Systems

But navigating and breaking through concrete barriers is only possible when we keep our sympathetic nervous system in check and strengthen our parasympathetic nervous system. Our sympathetic nervous system is responsible for fight-or-flight responses—it helps to promote survival by releasing adrenaline into our systems, allowing us to flee or fight when we're faced with a threat.

But survival isn't only the responsibility of the sympathetic nervous system. Responsible for promoting digestion and reproduction, the parasympathetic nervous system is sometimes called the feed-and-breed response. Our parasympathetic nervous system allows us to stay cool, calm, and strategic in the face of threats. That's why it's key to organizing against racism. By practicing mindfulness, we can strengthen this system, better preparing us to march for justice like our ancestors of the Civil Rights Movement.

The Power of Acceptance

Finally, we can strengthen our ability to advocate for ourselves and others through acceptance. When we accept America's history of racism, we acknowledge our own strength and that of our ancestors. Acceptance doesn't mean forgiveness—and sometimes forgiveness is a counterproductive response. But acceptance allows us to channel our anger in healthy directions, staying clear-headed and strategic like Mufasa.

Embracing Your Strength

By identifying concrete barriers, remaining calm in their face, and accepting their presence, we can help strengthen our transgenerational resiliency. This is the key to successfully navigating the threats we face and using them—just as our ancestors did—to further empower ourselves.

In the next section, I'll guide you through recognizing the power of your inherent strength and embracing your multi-generational identity.

PART FOUR

THE MULTI-GENERATIONAL SELF

CHAPTER 11
MULTI-GENERATIONAL TRANSMISSION

"THAT BOY'LL EITHER BE dead or in jail before he turns nineteen."

I can't count how many times I heard that statement. By the time I was eighteen, I was a known troublemaker. My family and friends all knew my reputation. With a taste for partying, I was willing to do just about anything for the lifestyle I wanted—except work for it. No matter how many people told me I was on the wrong path, I was determined to keep doing what I was doing. Lots of people tried to save me. I refused to listen.

It didn't take long for people to stop trying.

But one woman—my aunty Gwenny—refused to give up on me.

Shortly after my eighteenth birthday, I'd stolen some cash from my grandmother's wallet. I know it was wrong, and I knew it then, too. But I didn't care. With the cash in hand, my friends and I got so drunk and high that we didn't know which way was up. I passed out on my friend's floor that night.

I woke up early the next morning to my aunty Gwenny's fists. That morning, she'd found out about the cash I'd stolen. She was furious. After storming into my friend's house, she picked me up off the ground and started punching me—hard. I should clarify that I love my aunty Gwenny. She's always been my favorite family member.

And while she's obviously a pretty tough woman, there was no way I would ever hit her back. I wouldn't even dream of it. So as she pummeled me, I had no choice but to stand there and take it. My aunty Gwenny literally kicked my ass.

Eventually, she stopped hitting me and pointed toward the door. "Get in the car," she commanded.

If you've ever encountered a hungover eighteen-year-old, you can probably picture my reaction. I slumped my shoulders and pouted.

My pathetic huff went unacknowledged. "Now."

Still wearing last night's clothes, I marched dutifully out to her car and climbed into the passenger seat, eyes squinting against the morning sun.

"I took the day off," she said. "Because I'm not gonna let you ruin your life."

That's when I knew things were serious. An hourly worker, days off were precious for my aunty Gwenny. I kept my mouth shut as we rode in silence to a rundown strip mall. The sign in the window of the storefront read, "Be all you can be."

I stared at it in disbelief.

"Come on," she ordered. When I didn't move, she insisted. "You're going in there whether you like it or not. I don't give a shit about which branch, but you will join the military. It's not a request."

I literally had no choice.

As a teenage kid, I thought it was totally unfair. I was mad—fire-raging-in-my-gut mad. I was scared, too, and mostly I just didn't want to go in there. I didn't want to join the military—I wanted to keep living the life I was living, no matter the outcome. I didn't care if it meant I would end up "dead or in jail," as my family said.

But my aunty Gwenny *did* care. She cared a lot. That's why she took off work and made me enlist—because she saw the path I was on, and she refused to let her flesh and blood continue down that road.

She was right about all of it.

That single action changed the course of my life. It saved me. Back then, I hated hearing people say I'd be dead or in jail, but, looking back, I'm not sure they were wrong. And I know, without a doubt, that aunty Gwenny was right.

My aunty Gwenny's actions can teach us a lot about multi-generational transmission. The final piece of the transgenerational resiliency puzzle, multi-generational transmission is the "nurture" part of the nature-nurture pair. It's about the lessons we learn from the previous generations—our recent ancestors—even when we don't want to learn them.

This is a key aspect of transgenerational resiliency, because, very often, African American children, teenagers, and even adults don't realize the power we carry in our genes. And when we don't see ourselves as the products of multi-generational perseverance, we easily underestimate our own potential. We give in to anxiety. We accept failure. And, as the eighteen-year-old me did, we believe the stories others tell about us.

I was angry at aunty Gwenny for a while. But eventually, I realized that she had taught me the most important lesson of my life—that I was stronger, smarter, and more resilient than I thought.

That power was always in my genes, but I didn't know it. I needed her to wake me up.

THE ROLE OF NURTURE

The psychological theory of multi-generational transmission suggests that certain behaviors and attitudes are passed down from one generation to the next. This can happen through various means, such as family dynamics, cultural traditions, or even simply observing and imitating those around us.

First coined by psychologist Richard Nisbett in the 1960s, the original multi-generational transmission theory focused on how attitudes and values are passed down from one generation to the next. He found that children often adopt their parents' attitudes, especially when those attitudes are reinforced by grandparents, aunts, uncles, and other family.

Multi-generational transmission often centers negative behaviors and attitudes, such as alcoholism or abuse. But, as in the case of transgenerational resiliency, it also holds tremendous potential for positive change—and that's how I like to think of it.

To truly understand how we can harness the power of multi-generational transmission, it's helpful to think of it as a process.

We know that all African Americans are born with resiliency in our genes. Because our ancestors survived unthinkable hardships, we have the capacity to persist in the face of challenges. But, when it comes to ethics, values, and morals, babies of all races are born blank slates. These traits are learned as we grow and develop.

As children, we first learn about culture and values from our families. We gradually enter the world through family friends. And then, when we start school, we encounter a whole new set of ideas. This is a quiet form of cognitive restructuring. Unlike the intentional restructuring done through therapy and exercises like those you've completed in this book, multi-generational transmission is an unintentional form of learning. And we do it all the time.

Sometimes, we observe behaviors that reinforce our previous beliefs. Those observations strengthen—or myelinate—the connections in our brains. We watch our parents repeat their most typical behaviors over and over until they become natural to us. We simply don't know, as children, that there are other ways to live.

In other cases, particularly as we grow and encounter people outside of our immediate family, we notice behaviors that differ from our previous learning. These can be shocking at first, as when my aunty Gwenny drug me to the recruitment office, but they can become a new way of understanding the world. And, to become our new understanding of the world, they have to be reinforced often enough to myelinate.

Recall that African American transgenerational resiliency has encoded strength in our genes. This means that, as we encounter behaviors that reflect power, confidence, and perseverance, they are more easily myelinated in our brains. So even if we observe actions that are negative or ultimately harmful—even if we participate in those choices ourselves—we have the ability to filter them out and choose more positive life courses.

For example, all children grow up with some sense of work ethic. Regardless of who raises us, we see what they have to do to keep food on the table and clothes on our backs. We learn about work ethic, and we carry it through our lives. Whether we choose to become lawyers or teachers or police officers or factory workers, the work ethic is the same—and we learned it by watching the adults around us when we were very young.

That's multi-generational transmission. Sometimes called nurture, multi-generational transmission reflects learned behaviors as opposed to the traits we're born with.

Even though they are framed as opposites in nature versus nurture debates, multi-generational transmission and transgenerational resiliency aren't separate from one another. They're complementary.

Think of the first time you were called the n-word.

Maybe you went home and told your family what happened. If you were really young, maybe you didn't even know what the word meant. Or maybe you hid the experience from your family. Either way, I bet it came out eventually.

I'll bet, too, that your parents weren't surprised. They were probably angry and sad, and they may have thought you were too young for the experience, but I doubt it caught them completely off guard.

No African American parent is shocked the first time their child is called the n-word, because they experienced the same thing as children. Their parents did, too, and so did their parents' parents.

So when you told your family that you'd been called the n-word, they may not have been calm—but they weren't surprised. They probably drew on their own experiences, modeling the behaviors of their family when *they* were first called the n-word. And, however they reacted, they showed you—through their actions—how to process the experience.

They didn't let it break you.

This is the perfect example of how multi-generational transmission feeds transgenerational resiliency.

On one hand, they knew how to react because they'd seen others react. They'd had the same experience years before, so they knew what you were feeling. And, whether or not they effectively explained it to you, their reaction helped coach you to keep your head up and not let the experience crush your spirit.

They modeled particular behaviors for you. They taught you how to react in a way that allowed you to keep living your best life.

That's multi-generational transmission.

But, on the other hand, even without your family's modeling, the experience couldn't break you. You have strength in your DNA, so you were bound to survive.

That's transgenerational resiliency.

MY MOTHER'S GRIT

I don't know if I fully appreciated the power of multi-generational transmission until I was studying to be a psychologist. As I noted early in this book, there was a lot of White Psychology in my training program. The white professors in my program talked a lot about transgenerational trauma, and, one day, a professor told the class that it impacted Black communities to the point of threatening our survival.

At some point, I couldn't take it anymore. "What do you mean?" I asked.

I thought I saw the professor's face redden, but he answered confidently. "I just mean that transgenerational trauma can be so severe that families aren't able to improve their situations. They just give up."

I cocked my head to the side. "I never saw my mother give up," I said, my voice steady, "Actually, my mom worked three jobs so that I could go to an all-white school."

Now the professor looked dumbfounded.

"My grandparents built their own house. Yeah, life wasn't perfect. We were poor. But they had an amazing work ethic—it brought me to where I am today."

We've already discussed the problems of White Psychology and transgenerational trauma—there's no need to rehash that point. But it's worth noting that my mom wasn't traumatized. Neither were my grandparents.

They taught me to work hard for what I wanted, but more than that—they taught me how to allow the world's difficulties to bounce off me. They taught me that, no matter what society throws at you, it's your choice whether it sticks.

I think about that moment a lot. It was an opportunity for me to share my family's triumphs in more ways than one—not only did I literally tell the class about the life my family built for me. I also demonstrated—modeled—what true resiliency looks like. I kept a clear head and simply told the truth.

I've always been grateful for my mother—for my family in general—but that moment forced me to realize how much I inherited from her.

People talk a lot about single mothers, usually with pity or judgment. But my mother gave up so much to raise me. She dedicated her life to helping me become an adult, lifting me out of the hood and putting me through high school.

Some days, when I feel tired or worn down, I'm not sure how she did it. She walked through the ice and snow to get us to my basketball games. Sometimes, we took four buses to get to where I needed to go to succeed.

That professor went on to say that single mothers struggle to keep their families going—he argued that they aren't able to do what is needed to maintain a stable home life.

But my mom did what she had to do. She went to work in the heat, the cold, the ice, and the rain. When she didn't have access to a car or a ride, she took the bus. She stood on her feet too many hours and slept too few.

Maybe some people see that as a tragedy. I see it as evidence of incredible strength, a powerful black queen on the chess board.

I see it as transgenerational resiliency.

EXERCISE: HOW WERE YOU NURTURED?

Multi-generational transmission is deeply ingrained in us. That means it can be difficult to identify the experiences we've had that taught us how to live our lives. But without focusing on the gifts our recent ancestors gave us, we can't fully appreciate our transgenerational resiliency.

In this exercise, you'll reflect on the powerful lessons you've learned from the people who raised you. Even if your childhood wasn't a positive experience, I promise you that there are lessons to be learned about our generational knowledge from the things we observed as kids.

This exercise will combine mindfulness, visualization, and talking or writing about your thoughts. As you go through the exercise, use your knowledge of techniques from previous exercises in this book. Remember that the most important aspect of any exercise is letting go of your preconceptions and allowing your mind to wander without putting limits or boundaries on the ideas, thoughts, and emotions that arise.

Visualization

Begin by visualizing the person most responsible for raising you. If you were raised by more than one person, you can always come back and repeat the exercise, but for now, focus on just one person. Write down or draw the following:

What is/was their name?

What is/was your relationship to them? When you picture them, what do you see? List at least five physical traits (e.g. tall or long hair) as well as five personality traits (e.g. contagious laugh, easily annoyed).

List at least five memorable experiences you had with that person. Some of these may be obviously significant (such as when my aunty Gwenny drove me to the recruitment office). Others might seem more trivial (a birthday party or a trip to the zoo). Don't filter your ideas. Just list them without judgment.

From the list you created, choose one experience that feels the most positive to you. Again, don't filter your choice based on what you think is the most significant. Go with your gut and choose the experience that feels the most positive.

Experience

Paying extra attention to the list of traits (from question three), read back through your list.

Close your eyes and picture the person.

Then, keeping your eyes closed, think of the experience you chose in question five. Allow the events to play in your mind like a movie—be sure to picture every detail you can remember. Imagine yourself back there, as vividly as you can, reliving the experience.

Explore

Now, answer the following questions. It's best to talk through your answers with a trusted friend or family member. If that's not possible, write down your answers or say them aloud to yourself.

What happened? Including as many details as you can, explain the situation.

Focus on the person you chose. What did they do?

What traits do their actions reveal? What was it about their identity that made them choose to do what they did? How do those traits show up in *your* identity?

What do you think you learned from the experience?

Reflection

Over the next few days or weeks, reflect on the lessons you learned as a child, teenager, or younger adult. Alongside the resiliency in your DNA, you also inherited the positive traits of the people who raised you. You probably had some negative experiences, too—you may have even lived through some terrible things. But I guarantee that someone has stepped in to support you at some point, even if it was after childhood, and that person gave you some powerful tools for living.

Embracing those traits can help us better connect with our own multi-generational identity. As we'll cover in the next chapter, this identity is a key part of our true transgenerational resiliency.

CHAPTER 12
KNOW WHO YOU ARE

IMAGINE AN ELEPHANT CHAINED TO A STUMP. Since birth, she's had that shackle around her ankle. Her mother and siblings are chained to stumps, too. Even though they are incredibly strong, they understand that they are held by chains. They find a way to survive, despite the restraints. With no experience living in the wild, the elephant just assumes the restraints are strong enough to hold her, so she never tries to escape. She has no way of envisioning a different life for herself—no way of knowing she's different from any other animal—horses or goats or dogs—who are effectively restrained by chains and stumps.

But she is.

Elephants are stronger than other animals, and, of course, much larger.

So why does the elephant remain chained to the stump when she could so easily break free? The answer is learned helplessness.

Learned helplessness occurs when we believe we are powerless to change our situation. Through constant reinforcement, the idea that we are hopelessly stuck in our current situation becomes myelinated —it becomes common sense.

But the important aspect of learned helplessness is in the name—

this type of self-restraint is learned. By immersing us in an environment that tells us we have no choices, no future, and no hope for change, society tells us that we are helpless.

Just like optimism and persistence, learned helplessness is created through particular connections in the brain. When we associate an action with a particular outcome—then repeat that to ourselves over and over again—the connection becomes myelinated. Learned helplessness occurs because we've connected thoughts of advancement with thoughts of impossibility. Through repetition, that connection grows so strong that we forget there was ever another option.

But that connection is far from the only option.

Imagine, after days, weeks, and months of watching her mother submit to her chains, that little elephant gets an idea. She decides to explore. Seeing a brightly colored flower or a particularly tasty leaf in a clearing just out of reach, she pulls a bit at her chain. And it gives. It moves just a little at first, but the more she tugs, the further the stump rises until the very edge of the roots sticks out of the ground. With one more tug, she's free.

But what comes next is the truly remarkable part. By realizing her strength, the elephant not only freed herself—she also demonstrated the pathway to escape for the other elephants. They had no way of knowing, before that day, what they were capable of, but with one small act of strength, they can finally see a future unchained.

That future isn't about running away, and it's definitely not about accepting the way things were. It's about claiming their home. No longer chained to someone else's land, when they break free, they can proudly take over the land as their own. The inspiration for their escape—for taking charge of their lives—came from that one little elephant. However, the *ability* to redefine their future came from their natural strength, power, and size.

It came from their identity.

I've seen African Americans fall into the same trap as the elephants. When we believe what society tells us about ourselves—

that we're destined for prison or death—we can easily forget our resiliency. We can't see the power we carry in ourselves, carefully passed down from our parents, grandparents, great-grandparents, and our ancestors since the beginning of time.

When we focus too much on the concrete barriers, it's easy to forget who we are. That makes it even more important that we remember our multi-generational selves. By focusing on our identities —the power and resiliency we've inherited through epigenetics and multi-generational transmission—we can do amazing things. We just have to remember who we are.

Just like the little elephant, we can begin with a simple exploration and end by freeing ourselves from our self-imposed limitations. That doesn't mean everything will be perfect—there will still be barriers in our way. But it does mean that we will face those barriers with all our strength, ingenuity, and power.

When we remember who we are, we remember our power. And that makes it impossible to feel pessimistic. That's the only way we can maintain our optimism, even when things look difficult—or even impossible.

We can only do it by knowing who we are.

THE IDENTITY KEY

You are a powerful, strong, resilient African American. I know that without even meeting you. Because your ancestors survived unthinkable hardships, morphing their DNA and their perspective on raising children, you have everything you need in your body.

By this point in the book, I hope you realize that. But I know well that you might not.

As I mentioned earlier in the book, I do a lot of work with the prison system. Many of my clients are on parole—and part of their parole is coming to see me. Mostly African American men, these guys never miss an appointment.

Sometimes I think the prison's managers wish they would. In my meetings with the higher-ups, I often hear disparaging comments about the men I work with. They complain constantly about how my clients didn't follow up

on something or didn't have a good enough attitude. "Alright," I'll say. "Then I'll see him twice this week."

Every single time, the response is something negative.

They tell me I'm wasting my time. They roll their eyes and tell me that these men—strong, resilient, brave African American men—aren't worth the effort. They'd prefer to throw them away, to recycle them through the system over and over until they die.

I won't stand for it.

I tell them that they should have a better attitude. But I save the majority of my energy for my clients, and for good reason.

Real change doesn't come from external forces—it comes from inside.

When I work with these men, I help them realize who they are. I help them see that they have generations of amazing African American ancestors whose DNA has given them superpowers. By working through the same exercises in this book, they discover how resilient they are, having survived five, ten, fifteen, or even twenty years in prison—years that would have broken lesser men and women. When they realize that and when they realize who they are—things start to change for them.

Not all at once, of course—they still face concrete barriers in employment, housing, and finances. But what changes before my eyes is their optimism.

These men never miss an appointment.

My office is in Southern California. In the summer, the desert temperature reaches 100 degrees or more. Sometimes I receive calls from my clients saying that their ride bailed on them. Many people would call that good—the friend who had offered to drive them to their appointment ditched them—it was totally out of their control, right?

But that's not what they say.

"I'm gonna be late today," they tell me. "Imma walk, so it's gonna take a while, but I'll be there."

At first, I wasn't sure what to say—when it's really hot, that walk is miserable and long, and they're not likely to make it before my next appointment arrives. Then I realized: walking to my office is their way of taking charge. They can't control whether their ride shows up. But they can control what they do about it. They can, at the very least, show their face in my office, demonstrating a good faith effort to grow.

That notion is the core of knowing who you are, because knowing who you are means knowing what you're capable of. It means understanding the system—the chess board, as we've discussed previously—and your place in it. It means knowing that you can move in ways that give you an advantage over the white players, but that there will always be concrete barriers to look out for. And, most of all, it means knowing that your ancestors prepared you to handle those challenges.

This became very clear to me a few years ago. The Obama administration had announced that Harriet Tubman would replace Andrew Jackson on the $20 bill. Tubman, of course, escaped enslavement in 1849 and became a "conductor" for the Underground Railroad, helping others to escape as well. Andrew Jackson, on the other hand, enslaved over one hundred African Americans in addition to causing the deaths and displacement of thousands of Native Americans from their land. The choice to replace Jackson with Tubman was a no-brainer to many.

But when Donald Trump took office, the idea went out the window.

Many people responded with righteous anger and cynicism. And while that anger was not misplaced—the situation was infuriating—there wasn't much the average person could do about it.

We can't control the system. We can work together to make change, of course, but we can't individually do much about the concrete barriers we face across our country.

But what we *can* do is control the way we feel about our potential—

we can direct our energy toward our growth and development and, therefore, affect our potential earnings. We can control how we approach earning money, whether those bills have our ancestors on them or not.

The only way we do that is by controlling our emotions, our mindsets, our optimism, and our positive thinking. Through those tools—the tools you've been practicing through this book—we can propel ourselves forward in a way that makes a much larger change than being angry about Tubman's place on American money.

When we focus on the concrete barriers, we lose our optimism. We can't ignore the barriers, either. The only solution is to embrace our strength and resiliency as we face those barriers. We are more than capable of navigating them—if we just remember who we are.

BILL RUSSELL AND THE POWER OF KNOWING WHO YOU ARE

Bill Russell is known as one of the best defensive basketball players of his generation. A long-time center for the Boston Celtics—during a time when the team dominated the NBA—Russell was named an NBA MVP five times, and an NBA All-Star twelve times.

But Russell's journey wasn't easy.

As a child growing up during Jim Crow, he saw his parents struggle through horrific acts of racism, even moving to a new place in the projects to escape the constant abuse. His journey to professional basketball was just as difficult—as a college player, he endured racist taunts and, at least once, was denied a place to stay while on the road with the team. And, as he rose through the ranks as one of the top players at the time, things didn't improve much. Russell believed that being the best player—and Black—made him a target.

And yet, he refused to forget who he was.

He repeatedly told others that he would not be a victim. Rather than dwell on the concrete barriers he faced, he knew who he was—a strong, smart, talented player with the power of generations of ancestors behind him.

The racist abuse still affected him—of course it did. But those external forces weren't as strong as his internal drive—racist fans, coaches, and white people in his everyday life could never define him. Because he wouldn't let them.

This is the power of knowing who you are.

And, because Russell knew who he was, he didn't stop with being good. He took control of his life, his sport, and his career and became better with each passing season. Eventually, Russell took on the role of player-coach for the team, and, in 1966, he became the first African American head coach in NBA history.

Russell could have believed the horrible things racists said about him from his childhood. But if he'd sunk into believing what others said about him, he wouldn't have been able to rise above and make change.

Like the elephant, he knew who he was. He knew that the chains of racism weren't powerful enough to stop him—because he carried the resiliency of generations in his blood.

And, like the elephant, his accomplishments weren't just about him. His success on and off the court paved the way for other amazing African American athletes and coaches. In fact, Russell played an active role in the Black Power movement, publicly standing with Muhammed Ali and taking on the nickname "Felton X," combining his middle name with the "X" that many Black Power activists used to replace their enslaver-assigned last names.

Russell didn't stop by just helping himself. He actively contributed to improving the lives of other African Americans through his activism.

But he also knew that his own internal growth was a force for change. By becoming the best of the best on the court, he could motivate others, demonstrating their power to break their chains.

He couldn't have done it without optimism. He had to believe he could make a change first. And, without knowing who he was—without recognizing his identity as a strong, resilient African American—he could never have conjured the optimism to fight back in the face of so many who wanted him to fail.

Identity is a powerful thing. As much as we all love to receive external validation, the only thing we can consistently control is our internal sense of self—our clear sense of our goals and values, and our relentless pursuit of personal growth and development.

Bill Russell knew that. It not only made him a star—it helped him change the world.

I AM FROM

In the last exercise, we considered how previous generations of African Americans shaped us through multi-generational transmission. This exercise builds on that idea by focusing on our identities, and how we personally incorporate our past experiences into our understanding of who we are today.

Adapted from George Ella Lyon's popular poem, "Where I'm From,"[1] this exercise will guide you through creating your own poem, showing the beauty of your past experiences—even if they didn't always seem positive at the time.

This exercise is particularly important to me. When I was training as a psychologist, I completed a similar exercise adapted from Lyon's poem. I found the experience incredibly powerful.

My Version

I am from the Midwest and Pennsylvania and hip-hop mixtape cassettes, recorded from the radio,

I am from "the sticks" and "the projects,"

From trains whose screeches sound like soothing white noise to my ears.

I am from a community of military veterans whose deaths motivated me to help others through mental health care,

From attending Freedom High School and Grand Canyon University.

I am from a single mother who worked daily to keep food on the table, and from a community who wouldn't give up on me,

And from Pittsburgh, Pennsylvania (Black and Gold) and East Coast Hip Hop (Wu-Tang and Biggie).

I am from a drug-infested community and from an area where Black men are told they must choose between death or jail.

I am from a family that produced a doctorate and a military combat deployed community.

I am from fried chicken and cornbread and hot cinnamon rolls on the weekends,

From sports in the snow all through the winter.

I am from those moments. I have developed my identity and I carry it in my professional and family life.

Your Version

Some aspects of my version of Lyon's poem may have resonated with you; others less so. But, in the end, this poem tells a powerful story about who I am and why everything that's happened to me throughout my life brought me to where I am today.

Using the prompts below as a guide, create your own "Where I'm From" poem. Don't worry about making the poem "good"—the purpose isn't to become a great poet. Instead, focus on the aspects of your life that have most shaped who you are, and do your best to write them in the spaces below or in a notebook or digital document.

Template

I am from [where you grew up] and [a specific item from your childhood home],

I am from [a phrase describing your childhood home] and [more description of your childhood home],

I am from [a plant, tree, or natural item from your past] and [personify that natural item],

I am from [reason why you went into this profession], and [second reason you went into this profession],

I am from [school] and [achievement],

I am from [memory of growing up] and [second memory of growing],

I am from [city/town you were brought up in] and [second city/town you were brought up in],

I am from [negative thing you were told growing up] and [second negative thing you were told],

I am from [proud achievement for you, your family, or community] and [second proud achievement],

I am from [food from your family history] and [second food from your family history],

from [a memory or object you had as a child].

Reflection

Once you've completed your poem, read through what you've written. Pay attention to the powerful sense of individuality you bring to the page, embracing who you are and how your experiences brought you to this point.

Remember that knowing who we are is the key to embracing our resiliency—and we can't know who we are unless we acknowledge our experiences, good and bad, and how they have shaped us so far.

Every once in a while, I revisit my poem. It never fails to inspire me. I encourage you to keep your version somewhere you'll see it often. Let it remind you of your transgenerational resiliency.

In the next chapter, we'll build up our resiliency even more by combining our past experiences with new goals. Just as the little elephant led the way for others to break free from their chains, we can guide others—and we can also follow others to become even stronger in our strength, optimism, and resiliency.

CHAPTER 13
MIRRORING THE STRONG

MY KIDS and I have a tradition. Any time we throw away a piece of paper—junk mail, an old class assignment, or a completed grocery list—we wad it up into a ball. Arching our wrists, we raise the paper into the air and arc it toward the trash can with perfect free-throw form.

And we yell, "Kobe!"

Of course, I taught them to do that. They were still very young when the Black Mamba retired in 2016.

The youngest player to ever check in to an NBA game, Kobe Bryant was incredible. Intensely competitive—a trait I relate to—he always brought his best to the court. His work ethic was unmatched, and he always rose to the occasion when his team needed him most. In 2006, he was named the Most Valuable Player of the NBA Finals, having won five championships with the Los Angeles Lakers, including three in a row from 2000 to 2002.

My kids didn't know all that when we first started making Kobe shots. But they knew how important he was to me. I felt like I'd grown up watching him play—almost like he and I grew up together. I sunk into the couch to watch the Lakers play countless times. Game after game, I got to know Kobe's style. I grinned when he did his signature fade away. When he stood at the free-throw line, staring the hoop down with intense focus, I held my breath. I could almost feel the bend of his hips in my own body and the texture of the ball against my palms.

After a while, I could predict his movements—I could feel what he was about to do. The most brilliant plays unfolded on the screen and, even though I couldn't believe the talent I was seeing, I already knew where he'd go next. Our bodies were perfectly in sync, even though I'd never met him.

Every time I watched him play, my brain rehearsed what it must be like to be him—to know how to make every shot with ease. By the time he retired, I knew how to shoot like Kobe Bryant taking the game-winning shot.

I've watched him countless times. I know how he fades away. I know how he moves. I know how he arches his wrist.

Have I ever done it before? No.

Will I make the shot? Probably not.

But I know how to play like Kobe because I've practiced playing —many times—by watching him.

I'm not delusional—there's a psychological explanation for all of this. When we watch others succeed or fail, our brains naturally empathize with them. We feel the same emotions they feel simply by watching them.

We play back their movements through our brains as though the experience is our own.

I felt the same way when Obama was elected president. Because I know who I am—an African American man in a country that had never elected a Black president—I could never see myself in previous leaders. But when we elected Barack Obama, I experienced that victory like it was my own. Seeing him walk onto that stage with his family, accepting the honor of the highest office in the land, I felt what he was feeling—pride, excitement, and a little disbelief flooded through my body.

I wondered if that was how my grandparents felt when the Voting Rights Act passed. Or if my ancestors felt that way on Juneteenth—the day the last enslaved people learned they were free. And, later, when Kamala Harris became the first Black woman Vice President, I know so many African American women felt the same sense of empathetic pride.

Watching Obama become president connected me with African Americans across generations, because when I saw Obama's joyful expression, I felt what he was feeling—and I knew my ancestors must have felt that, too.

All of these instances have one thing in common—someone winning and someone else watching. Beyond just inspiring us to do and be better, though, there is an actual brain reaction that helps explain why watching someone do something amazing makes us feel like we're there—like we're the ones winning.

The reaction is something we all experience every single day, but most of us never give it a second thought. And at the heart of the experience are tiny cells called "mirror neurons."

THE MAGIC OF MIRROR NEURONS

Mirror neurons—like all neurons—are brain cells that transmit electrical impulses. We've discussed neurons before, when we talked about myelination, the process of forming strong currents between particular groups of neurons. But mirror neurons are special.

Mirror neurons fire both when we perform an action and when we observe that action being performed by others.

To fully understand what mirror neurons are and, more importantly, their role in transgenerational resiliency, it's helpful to reveal their origin story. Back in the 1980s, an Italian scientist named Giacomo Rizzolatti gave a monkey a peanut—actually, he and his team gave a lot of peanuts to a lot of monkeys. Then they used brain scans to watch how particular parts of the monkeys' brains responded to the food.

Completely by accident, they found something they never expected.

Every time a monkey picked up a peanut, part of its brain fired. But the monkeys' brains also fired when the *researchers* picked up the peanut.

The neurons worked in the same way whether the monkey picked up the peanut itself or watched someone else pick it up.

With the unexpected finding in mind, the researchers tried a few different actions. It wasn't just picking up a peanut that reflected from the researchers' bodies into the monkeys' brains—eating the peanut had the same effect. Almost unbelievably, when a researcher ate a peanut in front of a monkey, the monkey's brain fired as though the monkey itself had enjoyed the treat.

In essence, the monkeys' brains, like mirrors, reflected the behaviors in front of them.

Psychologists around the world began to replicate the experiment, and not only with monkeys. When the same experiment was performed on humans, the results held up.

Decades later, mirror neurons are well-established science—and an important part of being human. They're the basic building blocks of empathy, since they allow us to see what others are going through and feel it ourselves. For example, if we see someone else crying, mirror neurons in our brain fire, reminding us of what sadness feels like.

This process isn't limited to sadness. Whether it's fear, happiness, excitement, anxiety, or any other emotion that shows on someone's face or body, when we see someone experience an emotion, we feel it, too. Our brains get so caught up in the emotional state that the experience becomes a part of us.

When we see someone do something amazing, we feel a burst of excitement. It feels like *we* walked that tightrope, *we* drove that stunt car, and *we* sunk that layup. Even though we just watched from the sidelines, our brains literally share in their victory.

When the elephant in the previous chapter broke free of her chains, other elephants were watching. Their brains fired when she escaped, just the same way they would have if *they* had escaped. Suddenly, their entire lives changed.

Mirror neurons, then, provide the science behind our ability to forge new pathways. By watching someone break free from their chains, we feel their freedom. We can chase that feeling, using it to drive us forward to create our own freedom.

That's why mirror neurons are so important to understanding our power—they allow us to mentally *feel* what it's like to be successful. By experiencing that success, we can build optimism.

And optimism is the key to resiliency.

WHEN THE ALLEGORY OF THE CAVE FAILS

One of the least optimistic stories in the history of philosophy, Plato's allegory of the cave demonstrates how optimism connects—or fails to connect—with our mirror impulses. The story describes a group of prisoners held captive in a dark cave. Restrained in their seats, they can only stare at the cave's back wall. A bright fire glows behind them as their captors move puppets in front of its light, making shadows dance on the wall. The prisoners have no idea that people are moving puppets behind them—they just think the dancing shadows are reality.

But, in the allegory, one prisoner escapes. He races to the mouth of the cave. And suddenly, he knows the truth—the shadows were never reality. Reality is much brighter and more vivid than anything they'd ever known.

When he races back into the cave to tell the others, his eyes can't adjust. He'd been in the dark his entire life, and seeing the sun has effectively blinded him to the cave's darkness. Although he tries to explain what he saw to the others, they only know that he can't see—that escaping the cave means blindness and delusion.

In short, they don't believe him. They recommit to their belief that the shadows on the cave walls are the true reality.

When people hear the allegory of the cave, they focus on the prisoners who refuse to leave. The escaped prisoner comes back to the others, screaming, "Wait! This isn't real! What *I* saw was real!"

But he can only *tell* them what he saw.

I have a feeling that, if they could have seen him—if they could have watched as he discovered the new world, even without seeing it themselves—they would have believed every word.

But, because he could only *tell* them, they couldn't believe what he was saying.

That's why movies like *Malcolm X* and *Hidden Figures* are so important. When we watch these amazing Civil Rights leaders on screen, leading a movement before our eyes, our mirror neurons fire as though we were there. We feel what they feel. That emotional mirroring tells us what we can do—especially when we mirror people who share our African American identity.

That's why it's so important to know who we are. When we know who we are, we can see ourselves in these powerful African American figures. And when we see them doing amazing things, we know we can do them, too. We watch others like us doing difficult things, and our anxiety decreases.

That's not unique to African Americans.

But when we pair the powerful work of mirror neurons with our transgenerational resiliency, we gain a unique form of optimism. Throughout history, no matter what our country has thrown at us—dogs, firehoses, lynching, or segregation—we've been able to look to previous generations for a roadmap of how to keep moving forward. If they could get through that, we can get through anything.

It's all about paying attention to the people who have gone before us—for as long as African Americans have existed, we've been leading others to realize their resiliency and break free from their chains.

There's no better example of this than the long history of slave rebellions.

IT JUST TAKES ONE TO LEAD A REBELLION

As long as there has been slavery, there have been revolts. It's simply impossible to crush the human spirit to the point where groups of enslaved people *don't* rise up against their captors. America was no different.

Throughout American history, each new rebellion grew stronger and more notable, pushing the country toward the Civil War that would eventually emancipate all enslaved people.

We know that epigenetics and multi-generational transmission drove that effort, making each new rebellion stronger and more notable.

What often goes unnoticed, though, is the role of psychology in slave rebellions. None of these rebellions happened in isolation. Instead, using the same psychological tools we've discussed in this book, revolutionary leaders gained strength and resiliency from those who had come before.

And when we trace the way history's most famous slave revolts built on one another, we can truly see the psychological power of mirror neurons—especially when those neurons combine with the epigenetic power of transgenerational resiliency.

One of the most famous slave revolts was led by Nat Turner, a relatively well-educated African American preacher. In 1831, he led what is popularly called "Turner's Rebellion," leading a group of slaves to kill over fifty white enslavers. A remarkable aspect of Turner's rebellion was the sheer number of enslaved people he gathered together. As a powerful speaker, Turner was able to inspire over a hundred enslaved and free African Americans to band together to attack slave owners in Virginia.

Turner was later executed, but not before his rebellion brought attention to the immorality of slavery. Because he could read—and because he was a religious man—he used the Bible to argue that slavery stood in opposition to Christianity. This argument would become pivotal in political discussions surrounding emancipation.

Turner's rebellion directly influenced the end of slavery in America.

But, while Turner claimed that God came to him in a vision and told him to lead the rebellion, he didn't come up with the idea alone.

Turner and other enslaved people knew well that slave revolts had sprung up around the country. Inspired by small rebellions they'd seen as children and younger adults, many slaves had plotted to rise up against their captors. They'd gained courage from watching others rebel, and, with the help of their mirror neurons, they rehearsed the steps of pushing back against the concrete barriers they faced.

The Prosser brothers, Gabriel and Solomon, plotted a similar rebellion three decades before Turner. While this rebellion was doomed to fail, the planning is instructive. The Prossers organized a diverse group of rebels—they recruited not only African Americans, but Native Americans and poor white people, too. This diverse group of rebels may have inspired Turner's rebellion, as well as other large-scale uprisings that followed.

They planned to take James Monroe hostage, using the Virginia governor as a bargaining chip to negotiate freedom for the uprising's participants and their families.

Although storms disrupted Prosser 's rebellion, it ultimately succeeded. Though the Prosser's didn't achieve their goal, they succeeded in fueling Turner's uprising. They plotted a rebellion that led to other rebellions around the country and, eventually ended slavery altogether.

But, like Turner, the Prosser's borrowed from other revolutionaries, using the stories they'd heard and the actions they'd seen to guide their plan. The Prosser rebellion was, in fact, explicitly inspired by the Haitian Revolution.

Gabriel Prosser got word of the Haitian Revolution and found the action profoundly motivating. His revolution borrowed the Haitians' motto, "Death or Liberty." So just as Turner borrowed a page from the Prossers' book, the Prossers borrowed strength from the

Haitians who had revolted—and earned their freedom—just a few years earlier.

The Haitian Revolution, one of the most successful in history, aided Prossers' Rebellion through the vivid stories that spread across the American South. Hearing these stories was like a mental rehearsal for potential revolutionaries. The vivid stories, often told with animated gestures and colorful voices, allowed the enslaved to imagine fighting back—and winning.

Like links in a chain, the Haitian Revolution led directly to Prosser's Rebellion, which led to Turner's Rebellion and, eventually, the emancipation of all slaves. At the heart of these successful rebellions is a leader with a strong sense of who they are. Brought up by powerful Black men and women, these leaders have watched others persist. Their neurons mirrored the strength of their parents, grandparents, and others around them. And, through years of mental rehearsals, they built up the strength and resiliency to fight for justice.

THE MULTI-GENERATIONAL SELF: KEY POINTS

This section explored the multi-generational self. From the earliest African Americans to our parents and grandparents, we are all the products of our ancestors. And this combined identity works alongside the biological strength we gain from epigenetics to make us unstoppable.

Since the next section will focus on awakening our true potential for resiliency, let's review what it means to have a multi-generational identity.

Multi-Generational Transmission

We all learn about the world by watching others. Whether you grew up with your biological parent or parents, were raised by grandparents, or came up under different circumstances, we learn by watching other African Americans around us.

These previous generations teach us about strength, work ethic, grit, and perseverance—even when we don't realize it. To truly tap into our full potential, we must examine how previous generations have nurtured us, building on the natural strength encoded in our genes.

Identity

It's difficult to be optimistic when we don't understand our full potential. When we accept the stories others tell us about ourselves, we're like elephants chained to tree stumps—we could easily break free if only we knew our natural, inherited strength.

This is the power of knowing who we are. It not only helps us to tap into our strengths; it impassions us to lead others in the fight for justice.

All of this requires us to face—and embrace—our pasts, including the difficult parts. But when we do, we can feel truly optimistic about our potential.

Mirror Neurons

Through our optimism, we experience the full rewards of our mirror neurons.

These tiny cells fire electrical impulses not only when we accomplish something exciting—but also when we see others accomplish them. Activities as simple as watching a movie, attending a basketball game, or looking up a famous Black history speech on YouTube can help us excel in our lives by allowing our brains to rehearse our potential strength.

Our natural resiliency works together with our mirror neurons to prepare us for difficult things in our personal, social, and political lives. And, through our mirror neurons, we can see others changing the world—and prepare ourselves to do the same.

Realizing Our Strength

Our identities are complex, but the most important thing to realize is our strength. As African Americans, we have inherited resiliency through our genes and through the strong Black men and women around us. In the next section, we'll explore ways to bring all of this book's lessons together to fully activate our transgenerational resiliency.

PART FIVE

ACTIVATING TRANSGENERATIONAL RESILIENCY

CHAPTER 14
THE ACTIVATING FORCE OF IDENTITY

MY DAUGHTER CAME HOME CRYING one afternoon. She's usually a happy, well-adjusted teenager, so I was surprised to see her so upset. But when she told us she was crying about cheerleading, I was floored.

She'd been cheering for a few years at that point, and she loved it. She'd made good friends and she's quite talented. The squad had gone to different competitions as long as she'd been involved, and typically those events were highlights of the year.

So, I asked her why she was crying.

"Because they want my hair straight," she gasped. "And I'm not going to look like everybody else."

My daughter was in the minority on her squad, not only racially, but also in her rejection of straight hair. She'd voted against it. But it didn't matter. Since the squad had decided that straight hair was necessary for the competition, she felt she had to change herself. Even though she didn't want to straighten her hair—even though her hair would never look the same as the white girls on the squad—she believed that, since she'd been outvoted, she had to find a way to change herself for the activity. I couldn't believe what I was hearing.

The decision was so wrong, and yet, they'd convinced my daughter that she needed to go along with it.

Shaking my head, I asked, "What if you were Muslim, and you wore a hijab?"

"What?" she asked, tears in her eyes.

"If you were Muslim and you wore a hijab, would you have to take it off? You wouldn't look like everyone else then, right?"

She cocked her head at me the way teenagers do and replied, "That's different."

"Is it?" I asked. "They would still be asking you to change something important about yourself, right?"

She'd stopped crying now, and I could tell she was starting to feel annoyed. But teenagers will be teenagers, so I pushed a little harder.

"Are you required to have two pom poms?"

"Yes."

"What if you only had one arm? Would you be able to have two pom poms?"

"No," she replied.

"Alright," I told her. "Be you."

She considered this for a minute. But although she'd stopped crying, I could tell she wasn't sold on the idea of pushing back against the team.

A natural human instinct, we all want to feel accepted.

But if acceptance means changing who we are, then we aren't really being accepted at all.

So, I pushed my daughter just a little further.

"There's no way to look like everybody else, because you're *not* everybody else," I told her. "Look like you. They have to accept you for being you."

She looked at me, skeptical. "I mean it. You can't have straight hair. And if you straighten your hair, it's going to start curling as soon as you start cheering, right?"

"Yeah," she replied.

"And when you see the pictures, you'll be mad, won't you?"

She laughed a little at that. "Yeah."

I put my arm around my smart, talented, beautiful kid. "Make your hair the way you want it. They have to accept you for being you."

Something changed in my daughter that day. She came home devastated, upset that she wasn't like everybody else.

By the time we'd finished our talk, she seemed a little closer to embracing her identity.

Her permission slip was laying on the counter. Right then, I grabbed the letter and scrawled along the bottom, "my daughter will wear her hair the way that she wants to wear it. Contact me if you have questions."

When I looked at my daughter again, she was grinning. I could feel the change in her. She'd gone from tears to empowerment—from feeling like she needed to fit in to believing that, hell yeah, she could wear her hair however she wanted.

Sure, she could have straightened it. And maybe that would have made her look a little more like the others.

But the others don't have what she has. As African Americans, we have the force of our ancestors behind us. We are stronger, tougher, and more resilient because of what they survived. Just as my daughter inherited her hair texture from the generations before her, she also inherited transgenerational resiliency.

So while it might have been easier to give in to what the other cheerleaders wanted—her little version of society—she would have lost so much by giving in. The first step in activating our transgenerational resiliency is to embrace our identity as strong, multi-generationally empowered African Americans.

Others can accept us or not.

What's important is that we accept ourselves.

FOCUSING INWARD TO ACTIVATE RESILIENCY

Society is constantly telling us we're inferior. My daughter experienced this when her teammates told her, indirectly, that straight hair is preferable to her beautiful, natural style. When white people lock their car doors as we walk by, they're telling us that we seem dangerous—that, in their opinion, we're less human, even scary. And potential employers tell us we're not worthy of their time, effort, or employment when they refuse to speak with applicants whose names they perceive to be Black.

Many of us come away from these messages believing we need to change ourselves—we believe we should become somebody else. We try to get in the minds of white people, considering every little thing our culture taught us to do. We ask ourselves why our white boss wore that tie, why our white classmates' shoes are better than ours, and why we grew up differently from our white friends.

We believe if we can only make ourselves more like our white coworkers, teammates, or friends, we won't have to face concrete barriers. After all, white people don't face those barriers. If we can make ourselves more like white people, we think, the barriers will fall away for us, too.

But that will never happen.

Trying to make yourself into a white person—trying to make yourself into anyone else, regardless of race—doesn't remove barriers. It only keeps us from seeing them. Remember, our awareness of concrete barriers is an inherent strength for African Americans. It's part of our transgenerational power.

In the chess metaphor we discussed earlier, we are the black queen. The most powerful of all the pieces, we always move second, which has trained us to think simultaneously about our offensive and defensive possibilities. It's something the white pieces never have to consider, which gives us an upper hand in the game.

Uniquely aware of the game's rules, we anticipate the concrete barriers that will confront us along the way. And we adjust to win anyway.

When we try to play as white pawns, we give up our inherent, hidden advantage. We hide the chess board from ourselves, blocking our ability to defend ourselves. And, because we're pretending not to be black pawns, we also give up our *offensive* abilities—we lose our connection to our inherent power.

There's only one way forward. We have to embrace who we are.

When I play chess, sometimes people judge the way I look. Chess is a very white game. Most of the people who play are white, and they expect other players to be white, too—at least culturally.

But I'm not white, and I have no desire to be white.

So I sit down at the chess board wearing Jordans and a durag. Because I refuse to be ashamed of who I am.

I invite you to sit down at the chess table—whatever your version of the chess table is—exactly as you are.

Maybe you have a lot of tattoos. Maybe you like flashy earrings or false eyelashes. Maybe you have long fingernails or braids or an afro.

All those things make you who you are. So all those things make you stronger. It used to get in my head—I'd wonder if I might look better if I had the other players' shoes. Maybe I'd play better if I had his watch.

I know that's not true. The truth is, we only play better when we embrace who we are, and then march forward into adversity.

IDENTITY, OPTIMISM, AND PRESIDENT OBAMA

Embracing our identity isn't without consequences. Society pressures us to take on a white identity, and when we refuse to conform, we experience rejection and even violence. When we look back over history, we can see this clearly—from Henry "Box" Brown and Harriet Tubman to Martin Luther King, Jr. and Bessie Coleman, previous generations of African Americans have often faced unfair consequences when they embraced their true identities.

But when we embrace our identities in the face of those consequences, we can experience concrete barriers not as a restriction—but as a type of empowerment. We encounter the systems meant to block us, and we stand up even taller. It reminds us how strong, powerful, and resilient we are.

Those barriers only make us stronger.

As a kid growing up in Hawaii, Barack Obama knew that intuitively. Obama once called his family "a little mini– United Nations." Originally from Kenya, his father Barack Obama, Sr. was Black. But his mother, Ann Dunham, was white—and it was Dunham who primarily raised the young Obama.

In his memoir, *Dreams from My Father*, Obama recalls the first time he was called a racial slur. His friends were mostly white, and, during an argument in the locker room after a heated game of basketball, one of them flung the word at him to assert his power. Obama later felt that the other boy didn't even know what it meant—but he knew he could use it to hurt him. In that childhood moment, Obama punched the boy, breaking his nose, later warning him not to use the word again.

But it was an awakening for the future president. It forced him to reckon with who he was.

As a biracial child, he struggled to come to terms with the ways he heard race described. His African American friends would talk about "white people," and he would picture his mother and grandparents. Sometimes, his Black friends would imply that he didn't really fit in, since he enjoyed the privileges of having a white mother.

But Obama knew that he faced the same concrete barriers as any other African American. Regardless of his white family members, he would always be seen as a Black man.

Society told him that his Blackness was a bad thing. Thankfully, he found the power in his African American identity. Once he waded through the concrete barrier of others' judgments, he embraced who he was. That allowed him to recognize the potential blockages that stood in his way—and to embrace the resiliency of his ancestors.

After completing his undergraduate studies at Columbia University, he worked as a community organizer in Chicago. He then attended Harvard Law School, where he became the first Black president of the Harvard Law Review. In both of these roles, he placed his African American identity front and center—as a community organizer, he was inspired by the Civil Rights movement, and this experience was later cited as a reason for his election to the head of the prestigious Ivy League publication.

After several years as a civil rights lawyer in Chicago, Obama ascended through the senate to the role he is best known for—President of the United States. His campaign fully embraced his African American identity. One of his most famous speeches, delivered less than a year before Election Day, explicitly discussed African American history. It called the country to acknowledge the difficulties our ancestors faced.

In other words, Obama's campaign revolved around his Black identity.

If he hadn't embraced who he was—if he'd focused on being half Black, half white—he wouldn't have brought such a wave of enthusiasm to the polls back in November 2008. I'm not sure he would have won.

Obama's victory was more than just a presidential election, though. By winning the highest office in the nation, he also encouraged other African Americans to embrace their identities. His success worked a lot like the elephant who discovers that it is more powerful than the chains that hold it. As he climbed the political ladder, he not only increased his own strength and resiliency—he also became a model for others.

Because when we embrace our identities, we do more than simply empower ourselves. Identity is a powerful force that activates our transgenerational resiliency. Because this step requires us to be bold, it also inspires others to follow in our footsteps.

Obama knew this. He frequently addressed African American children throughout his presidency and continues to do so today, encouraging Black boys and girls to believe in their abilities—to embrace their transgenerational resiliency.

When we think of it this way, it becomes clear how transgenerational resiliency is an ongoing, powerful cycle. Each generation builds on the previous generation, both through epigenetically enhanced DNA and multi-generational transmission. So while Obama benefited from previous Black generations and the knowledge and strength of African Americans around him, he also became a catalyst for future generations.

Most of us will never be president. But by embracing our identities, we can become an inspiration for other African Americans while increasing our resiliency.

All it takes is a strong, unapologetic embrace of who we are.

EXERCISE: ACTIVATING IDENTITY

Activating your identity is as simple as celebrating who you are. Throughout the book, you've explored various parts of your background. Those background elements form a map of our transgenerational strength.

That map takes the form of a genogram.

A genogram is a type of family tree that provides a graphic representation of family relationships and dynamics. It goes beyond a traditional family tree by incorporating medical, psychological, and social information about the family.

The genogram helps identify patterns of behavior and interaction within a family, and to understand how these patterns may have developed over time. Additionally, the genogram can be used in family therapy, providing a way for the therapist to visualize the family's relationships and dynamics.

But while genograms are valuable for understanding family relationships and dynamics, they're often used to blame our ancestors for their faults rather than celebrating their victories.

In previous exercises, you've considered the concrete barriers your ancestors faced and how those barriers shaped their identities. In this exercise, we'll use the genogram format—adapted to better illustrate transgenerational resiliency—to put all of those experiences together.

Family Tree

Begin by drawing your family tree on a large piece of paper. Place a dot at the bottom of the paper, right in the center, and label the dot with your name.

Above that dot, draw two or more dots to represent the people who raised you. This might be your biological parents, or it might be others who parented you—it doesn't matter. For this exercise, the point is to indicate all of the people one generation above you.

For example, if you were raised by your mother and your stepfather but saw your father and stepmother occasionally, draw four dots on the second line—one each for your mother, father, stepmother, and stepfather.

Then, on the line above that—the third line—continue the process by mapping out your grandparents' generation. If you can't fill in all of the gaps, it's okay to leave blanks, but try to be as thorough as you can. Hopefully the previous exercises have guided you through some of these questions, including who your ancestors were, so that you can go back a few generations. You can also include people who were influential to you but who aren't related by blood—recall that multi-generational transmission isn't biological, so we can be shaped by family friends, church members, people at work and school, and other community members, too.

If you feel that someone has shaped who you are, include them in your genogram wherever you feel is most logical.

Concrete Barriers

Once you've mapped your ancestors, you can begin to draw in the core of your transgenerational resiliency genogram: concrete barriers and the epigenetic strength they create.

You've already noted the concrete barriers your ancestors faced. Back in Chapter Two, you listed past generations' struggles. Revisiting that exercise and your knowledge of your ancestors, literally draw the barriers faced by the previous generations of your family.

For instance, if your father spent time in prison, he may not have been able to see you as often as either of you would have liked. In that case, choose how you want to note this barrier on your map. You might draw a box around your father and label the box, "prison," or maybe it makes more sense to you to draw a jagged line between his dot and your own. However you choose to draw the barrier, your drawing and label should illustrate the hardships your father faced, both in his own life and in his ability to shape who you are.

Visit each of the dots on your genogram, notating the concrete barriers that that ancestor faced. Remember to be generous and optimistic—transgenerational resiliency requires us to consider the ways society has held African Americans back. So if you find yourself focusing on previous generations' mistakes, consider whether it might be beneficial to reconsider how some of their actions were influenced by social barriers.

Epigenetic Strength

Finally, once you're done notating the concrete barriers of all past generations, you'll add the most important component of your genogram: epigenetic strength.

You should have a piece of paper covered with dots as well as markings that represent barriers. Now, as the last step in your genogram, begin to draw lines of transmission. Connect each dot with the other dots they influenced. So, if you were raised by your mother and grandmother, you'd draw a line from your mother's dot to your dot and a second line from your grandmother's dot to yours. In that case, you'd also draw a line from your grandmother to your mother, since, if they raised you together, your grandmother's wisdom probably also influenced your mother.

These may not be as neat or predictable as a traditional family tree. Since we're tracing much more than just bloodlines, there is likely to be some overlap as well as some dots that seem to connect with every other dot on your genogram. That's fine. Your genogram isn't meant to look beautiful—it's meant to help you map your strength.

You may choose to draw your lines in ways that are more meaningful to you. For instance, you may want to color-code your lines, using red to indicate a very strong bond and light blue to show weaker connections. You may want some lines to be squiggly or broken while others are bold and heavy. Draw the lines in whatever way makes sense to you.

As you connect the dots on your page, note the barriers that the lines must pass through. In the earlier example of a father in prison, for example, the line connecting the two of you will have to pass through the concrete barrier of prison.

That's more than just symbolic. It's a powerful representation of the way concrete barriers shaped our transgenerational resiliency.

As you continue to draw connections between the dots on your genogram, reflect on the crossing of various lines and shapes. This is a map to your strength. It's a visual representation of how hard your ancestors fought to bring you into the world—and, through that fighting, the added epigenetic strength they encoded into their genes as a gift to you.

Reflection

When you finish your genogram, step back and look at the entire picture. Consider how it changes your perception of yourself. What does it mean that your ancestors survived so much to bring you into the world? What can you accomplish when you combine their incredible power?

As you move through your day, practice embracing that identity. When you feel yourself being asked to change who you are, think back to your genogram and remember your power. Remember that changing who you are requires you to leave behind the powerful map you drew—and the even more powerful experiences it represents.

Draw from your ancestors' strengths and embrace who you are. You are powerful, strong, and resilient.

CHAPTER 15
THE OPTIMISM OF OUR ANCESTORS

MY SON MUST HAVE BEEN seven or eight when he first asked if he could be president. Kids that age ask questions all the time—"Is the Easter Bunny real?" "What jobs can I do?" "Why don't dinosaurs exist anymore?"

They're learning about their world.

We start gathering information about our environment at such a young age—especially before we turn seven. Since we build our perspective from that information, it's stubborn. The things we learn from our parents, teachers, friends, and people on television tend to stick with us. They make it difficult to change our mindset.

So as my son rattled through questions, asking which jobs he could have, I tried to be as optimistic as possible.

"Dad, can I be a doctor?" he asked first.

"Sure," I replied. "There are plenty of Black doctors."

He nodded. But as every parent knows, kids that age never stop at just one question.

Next, he asked, "Can I be a lawyer?"

I answered, "Yes." There are plenty of African American lawyers, after all.

He thought a little harder this time. "Can I be an astronaut?"

Searching my mind for the pictures NASA releases before each mission, I landed on the Challenger. I could picture him. There on the front row, all the way to the right, sat Ronald McNair, an African American scientist. "You can," I told him. "You know, you can do just about anything in America except be on a dollar bill." I thought for a moment. "Or, be president."

You can tell when kids that age are really thinking. For one thing, they get quiet—a rare occurrence. And, for another, their confusion is written all over their face.

My son narrowed his eyes. We've raised him to think for himself and, of course, to be very optimistic. So it hadn't even occurred to him that I would tell him he couldn't have a particular job.

Finally, he asked, "Why can't I be president?"

"Well," I replied. "Numbers don't lie, right?"

"Right," he said confidently.

"The United States has had forty-three presidents."

He nodded.

"And zero percent have been Black." I looked my son in the eye. As much as I hated telling him this, I believe in being honest and forthcoming with my children. So I pressed on. "So as smart and capable as you are—and you are very smart and very capable!—if we just focus on the statistics and numbers, you have a zero-percent chance of becoming president."

I'm not sure if he truly understood what I was saying or just wanted to play with his Transformers, but he simply nodded and ended the conversation.

Nobody likes to tell their kids they can't do something. But, up until that point, I didn't believe I could have been president either. Nobody who looked like me had ever held that position. So when Barack Obama came along, I wasn't sure he had a chance.

But Obama himself seemed to truly believe he could win. Soon, I believed it, too.

There was a point in history not so long ago when I would have had to tell my son he couldn't be an astronaut. It wasn't until 1983 that an African American went to space.

At one point, there were no Black lawyers, either. And before that, there were no Black doctors.

But each new generation brought a new, visionary African American into the world—one with a vision for what and who they could be.

And, like the elephant who broke her chain, that one person set out to become a historic first. It only takes one. Because when others see what's possible, they change their mindsets, too. They're sure to follow.

That one example can change our whole perspective, leading us to believe that even greater things are possible.

A decade after my son asked those questions, I had different answers. We'd had forty-four presidents by then; among them was an African American—a Black man optimistic enough to believe he could be the first.

So when my younger son asked whether he could be president, I told him, "Absolutely. You can be president."

He didn't even blink. He didn't hesitate. He just believed me.

But I wanted him to know how quickly things can change, so I said, "You know, I had this conversation with your older brother, right?"

"You did?" he asked.

"Yep. Probably ten years ago. I told him he could do anything but become president."

"Why?" he asked.

"Because our country had never had a Black president before," I replied. "But you—you could be president. And, you know what?"

"What?"

"Your brother could be president now, too."

With just one seemingly small breakthrough, the entire universe changed.

It would be easy to dismiss Obama's rise to office. In the end, one

African American president out of forty-six only amounts to about two percent. But I look at that number with optimism. After all, at one time only two percent of doctors were Black before that, the number was zero.

To grow those numbers takes optimism. Obama had to bring incredible optimism to his career—otherwise, he never would have run for president. Oprah began as a local news anchor. Michael Jordan was cut from his high school basketball team.

Many African American firsts began this way—one person who had a vision for their life, someone whose optimism was unbreakable.

It takes a lot to get there. From the time we're born, we observe the world to determine what's possible. I experienced that when my older son asked if he could be president—for the first thirty years of my life, the answer was unequivocally, "No."

But everybody's cognitive outlook—their morals, values, ethics, and beliefs—can be shifted by just one person. When just one African American historical figure shows us what can be—when they demonstrate their optimism and resiliency—they outshine everything else.

And that keeps us moving forward. It makes us unstoppable.

HOW OPTIMISM MAKES US UNSTOPPABLE

Optimism is the key to Obama's power—and Oprah's power, and Michael Jordan's power, and every other African American leader's power. We've talked about optimism before. It's the key to breaking the anxiety loop. If we use it correctly, it doesn't produce entitlement —it just helps us understand the power of struggle and reflect on what our ancestors have been through so that we may apply their strength to our lives.

But at its core, optimism is simple.

It's a belief—deep down—that we can do it.

And when we carry that belief into our daily lives, it becomes motivation. We place our dreams at the center of our lives and trust that we will accomplish them.

With that driving force, we have a reason to wake up in the morning.

But that reason isn't just our dreams. After all, if we had dreams we didn't believe we could accomplish, they wouldn't do much to motivate us.

The reason we wake up in the morning is our optimism. It's our belief we can do more than just dream—we can actually accomplish that dream.

Of course, optimism alone doesn't guarantee us a win. We might not achieve the thing we set out to do.

But even if you don't get that win, others will see you working toward your goal. That optimism seeps out of you because every morning, you jump out of bed and work towards that ultimate dream.

That's what it means to be unstoppable.

It's not about achieving every single thing you've ever wanted. History makes that very clear. As we've seen throughout this book, our ancestors were unstoppable—but if you asked them whether they'd achieved everything they ever dreamed of, they would probably laugh. Being unstoppable isn't about winning. It's about believing you can win and never giving up. It's about optimism.

And so, with each new day that we continue to work toward our goal, we grind away at those concrete barriers. At first, the damage is barely visible. Maybe a speck or two of dust falls away.

But eventually, there's a little chip in that hard, smooth surface.

And then a chunk of concrete crumbles in our hands. And maybe, if you're lucky, you punch a hole through the barrier. The block is still there, of course, but now others can see the promise of optimism.

They can see through the barrier. When that happens, other people grab their chisels. They come to work on the barrier alongside us, making the work easier and driving our optimism even more.

That's what Obama did. It's what Oprah and MJ did. They kept chipping away at those barriers until their optimism was contagious.

In more technical terms, these Black leaders helped us all restructure our brains. They went against everything we'd learned in our lives—everything that told us we couldn't be a president, a media mogul, or a billionaire athlete-turned-actor-turned-businessman.

When our neurons fired automatically, telling us we couldn't, their presence gave them pause. Their success made us stop and think about the assumptions we made about what we could do.

They crossed over the threshold from fear to freedom.

From the perspective of anxiety and optimism, that threshold is a big, big deal. It's a line in the sand that tells our brains to be careful—even though we are uniquely able to see the entire chessboard, we're approaching uncharted territory. When we see someone else cross that threshold, we know it's safe.

We know we can cross it our own way.

Our path might not look like Obama's. A brilliant scholar and charismatic thinker, he excelled in ways that might be inaccessible to you and me. And our path might not look like Oprah's. As an incredibly savvy businesswoman, she had a unique, important vision for her life.

But, while their concrete barriers were real, it wasn't just their particular skills that helped them overcome the roadblocks in their way—it was their optimism.

And when we see others plow through those barriers, we gain that optimism, too.

That optimism wasn't created by Obama or Oprah, though. It's inside of you, and it's been there since before you were born—it's in your DNA, just waiting to be activated.

Throughout this book, you've seen how our ancestors help us to see our power. That process begins with our identity. When we know who we are, that identity becomes a driving force in our lives.

But we also need the optimism that tells us our identities are powerful. By embracing our ancestors' optimism, we activate that piece of our transgenerational resiliency too.

That process doesn't stop when you finish this book. The most powerful way to embrace your inner strength, resiliency, and optimism is to look around you, acknowledging what your ancestors did. The more you see other African Americans doing amazing things, the more motivated you'll be to do those things, too.

You don't necessarily have to believe you can, at least not at first. Because simply seeing the power of Black Americans is enough to cognitively restructure our brains, activating our epigenetic power. Optimism is a side effect of that process—but it's also a driving factor in moving forward with our lives.

That optimism is precisely what our ancestors had. By embracing it, we walk in their footsteps, each of us becoming our ancestors' proudest, most ambitious dream come true.

And through that process, we step into the role of our ancestors. We get out of bed every day determined to make a change in our lives —and the world. And by doing that, we gather others to our cause.

This has always been the pattern of African American resiliency. And it's right there in your DNA, just waiting to be switched on.

EXERCISE: OUR ANCESTORS' OPTIMISM

In the previous chapter, you mapped your identity. That genogram told you everything your ancestors did to make sure you were strong. Through their optimism, they poured resiliency into you. It became part of who you are.

That exercise helped you to see all the things your ancestors overcame for you. By visualizing the concrete barriers that fell between you and previous generations, you saw how unique and powerful your identity is—how far it can take you toward your goals.

But it can be difficult to truly recognize what our ancestors overcame. The further back in history we go, the less we can really understand what some of their struggles meant. We've seen our own concrete barriers. But some of the barriers our ancestors saw are—thankfully—unimaginable to us today.

And yet, we must imagine them.

To truly understand who we are and what we are capable of achieving, we have to imagine the things our ancestors went through. It's the only way we can imagine ourselves overcoming our concrete barriers. It's how we zoom out to give ourselves a view of the chessboard.

So in this exercise, we'll build a mental image of our ancestors as they chipped away at the barriers they faced. That image, as you've learned, can help us to build optimism. It can activate our resiliency by prompting us to cognitively restructure our view of the world.

Choose Your Stories

Begin by choosing a few of the stories you've gathered throughout this book.

Looking over your genogram—as well as any notes you've taken in previous chapters—list four or five specific concrete barriers that speak to you. These could be huge, seemingly impossible blockades, or they might simply be scenarios that remind you of your own struggles. You might even have some of both.

Jot your ideas down in just a phrase or two—"Grandad in prison" or "Great-aunty Harriet fighting to vote."

List Your Dreams

Now create a new list. This list isn't about your ancestors—it's about you.

Write down four or five of your biggest dreams. Try not to limit yourself to just what you think is easily accomplishable. Think big.

Depending on where you are in life, you might list things like, "write a book," "save up for a mortgage down payment," or "finish my degree." It's okay if you find yourself thinking these things are impossible. In fact, you should probably be a little scared—those dreams would require you to cross the threshold between fear and freedom!

Compare Your Lists

Look at your two lists. Do you see any similarities between the two? Perhaps you want to run for political office and you have an ancestor who participated in the Civil Rights movement. Or maybe you want to earn a master's degree and your father was the first in your family to go to college.

Try to find a parallel between two of the items on your list, even if the link is a stretch.

Circle those two items.

Tell Their Story

Beginning with the historical example you chose, draw or write your ancestor's story. Try to be as detailed as possible. While you shouldn't worry about making the story "good," you can use a beginning, middle, end structure to guide you.

Start by describing what their life was like before the challenge. That part is the beginning of their story. If you chose to draw the story, this can be a panel, like in a comic strip. If you're writing, you'll probably mostly write descriptions. Where did they live? What kinds of things did they do for fun? What was their personality like? Who did they love? Where did they work? What was their job?

Then describe the incident itself. Where did it happen? What were they wearing? How did they feel? Who else was there? If you're drawing a picture, make the image as vivid and detailed as possible. Try to imagine the pain they must have felt as they worked through the issue, but imagine the optimism, too. What made them believe they could overcome this barrier?

This section will probably be longer than the last, and, if you chose to draw the story, you may need to break it into multiple panels. Do whatever you need to do to get a solid, detailed image on the page, either through words or pictures. Finally, finish with the end. If your ancestor survived the barrier, draw or describe how they looked and felt afterward. Use plenty of detail here. While we all feel happy when we achieve a goal, other feelings also come up. Did they experience disbelief? Were they afraid of backlash? If so, how did they deal with that? Did they celebrate? Did they tell their children, other family members, or friends? What happened after they'd broken through that barrier?

Draw or write the end of the story.

Reflection

When you finish, read or look back over your work. You should see the strength and optimism of your ancestor—after all, they couldn't have achieved their goal if they weren't optimistic enough to try.

Tell Your Story

Now, complete the same exercise for your own challenge.

Unlike your ancestor, you haven't yet overcome this obstacle. But you, too, must be optimistic if you hope to accomplish your goal.

So imagine yourself like your ancestor. As you write or draw the beginning, middle, and end of your journey, reference what you wrote for them. How can the things they experienced inform what you'll experience? How can their strength guide your own?

Pay particular attention to the final panel or section—this section describes how you'll feel when you accomplish your goal, and it's particularly important. After all, optimism isn't just about believing we should try. It's about believing we can win.

Reflection

When you've finished, keep your story—and your ancestor's story—somewhere you'll see it often. If you chose a work-related goal, keep your story in your workplace. If it's related to your home life or other personal aspirations, keep it in your home, somewhere meaningful where you'll see it often, especially when you're thinking of your dreams.

Even if you never knew the ancestor you drew, their strength, wisdom, and optimism can help you to activate your own.

Use the story—along with your genogram—as a template for your own success. And remember, by embracing your transgenerational resiliency, you are very likely activating it in others.

CHAPTER 16
FINDING YOUR GRIT

DAVID GOGGINS DIDN'T ALWAYS REALIZE how strong he was. After an incredibly difficult childhood, he floated from a stint in the Air Force to a job as an exterminator. He had no passion for either of them. As the years went on, his weight got out of control, and at nearly three hundred pounds, he felt far older than his years.

With little motivation to do much else, he spent a lot of time watching television. One day, he saw a TV show about Navy Seals. He was inspired. As he watched the program, transfixed by the Seals' passion and bravery, he made a decision.

He would become one of them.

But he faced one major problem—to qualify for service, he would have to lose one hundred pounds. And yet, he refused to give up. He set out to become an elite athlete, limiting his caloric intake to less than a third of what he'd been eating. And he started exercising. Hard.

He eventually completed an ultra-marathon—a 100-mile race. When he recounts this experience, he doesn't seem phased by the lost toenails or the painful muscle cramps. He survived something most people never even attempt, and the experience made him stronger.

What Goggins didn't realize was that the strength to lose weight, get in shape, join the Seals, and become an elite athlete was always in his DNA. But when he decided to push himself, he activated his transgenerational resiliency.

He found his grit.

Even though the strength of his ancestors was always inside him, he had to dig down deep to find it. When he did, his power was unstoppable.

I think of it like a wildfire.

Fires don't just start on their own. Every fire begins with a spark. But when a forest gets dry, the tiniest flicker can set the whole thing aflame. That fire spreads, igniting dry leaves and other kindling, before catching one tree, then two more, then a dozen, until the entire forest burns.

That type of fire doubles and triples itself as it spreads.

That's why wildfires are so difficult to contain.

Transgenerational resiliency is like that.

The potential for fire is always inside of you. At the tiniest spark, it ignites. And from there, refuses to be contained.

But what does it take to light that first fire? What does it mean to find your grit?

The answer is simple: knowledge.

David Goggins couldn't have known the power he had in his DNA. If he had, he wouldn't have settled for an unhappy life in the first place. I meet a lot of people like him in my line of work—people with power in their blood who don't even realize the strength and resiliency they carry inside.

They sleep on all that power, letting themselves get sucked into the anxiety loop, ignoring the mental strength they've developed all their lives without even realizing it.

But like Goggins, most people I work with eventually come to see what they have. We talk about transgenerational resiliency—the power they have encoded in their genes—and eventually, they discover their strength.

That little bit of knowledge is all it takes to spark a fire. Simply by knowing their potential strength, they can move forward, using positive psychology to change their lives.

From that point forward, nothing can break them.

That doesn't mean they don't struggle. Our ancestors left us the gift of strength, but we still have to face plenty of concrete barriers. But with transgenerational resiliency, we encounter those challenges with optimism. Whether we want to run a marathon, go to college, become postal workers, or buy a house, we face the challenges ahead and refuse to break.

Those challenges aren't fatal. They're simply an opportunity to restructure.

All of that is as simple as learning about what's inside us.

And the best part? You already know it's there.

You just have to put it into practice.

HARNESSING THE POSITIVITY CYCLE

Earlier in this book, I wrote about the anxiety cycle. It usually begins with a tight feeling in your chest. You feel trapped and afraid.

The more anxious you get, the more your body reacts. And the more your body reacts, the more anxious you get.

It's what we call in psychology a "maladaptive cycle." Maladaptive cycles are our bodies' form of crossed wires—our brains respond to an unfamiliar circumstance the best way they know how. Unfortunately, the response itself stops us from getting comfortable with our new situation.

I don't bring this up to dwell on the problem of anxiety. We've already discussed how optimism is the antidote to anxiety. I raise this issue to demonstrate that cycles are for more than just anxiety.

We can harness a positivity cycle, too.

When we think about something, it stimulates our bodies. That's not only true of anxiety. As you know from my Kobe Bryant story, our bodies also use mirror neurons to feel what it's like to do something daring, bold, or just plain epic.

Think about the best day you've ever had—a day when you finally got something you'd wanted for a long time. Depending on where you are in life, that could be anything from your wedding day or the birth of a child to the day you found out you'd passed a really hard class or the first time you drove a car.

When you think of that day, I bet you feel something in your body. It might be a little tingle in your chest. It might be a grin that spreads across your face or a laugh that escapes unintentionally.

That feeling in your body is your brain preparing you for the challenges ahead.

It's the same response that's triggered in an anxiety cycle—our brain imagines a particular circumstance and prepares our body to follow through.

We just have to replace the anxiety cycle with a positivity cycle.

Think about how you feel when you get a fresh haircut or style. When you look in the mirror, you can't help but admire yourself. You look good and feel good, and a little wave of confidence washes over you.

It's hard to have a bad day after that.

For most of us, that little boost of confidence makes us feel happy, then that happiness translates to optimism. That optimism helps us move through our day, confident that we can achieve anything. When we feel that kind of confidence, we perform better. Our positivity becomes a self-fulfilling prophecy propelling us to positive results. And with every positive result, we feel even more optimistic.

It's the healthy version of the anxiety cycle. That feeling of positive psychology can't be stopped. From the moment the positivity cycle begins, positive things begin to occur because we believe they will.

When we believe positive outcomes can occur, we're more willing to take the necessary actions to achieve those outcomes. If we believe we can graduate from college, we fill out the application. If we don't, we won't. If we believe we can become a deejay, we order a deejay set from Amazon. If we don't, we won't. If we believe we can run a marathon, we start a training program. If we don't, we won't.

The secret is incredibly simple. When we feel better, we perform better. When we perform better, we get better results. When we get better results, we feel better. The cycle continues indefinitely, as long as we let it.

And the best way to get started is to remember what our ancestors did for us.

GRIT IN OUR DNA

A true positivity cycle begins with activating our sense of optimism. If you've been following along in this book, you've already begun to practice that optimistic outlook. But it can be challenging to get the cycle started.

Fortunately, our ancestors left us more than genetic strength and resiliency. They also left stories to inspire us.

When you think of the experiences your ancestors survived, you should feel a tingle of pride. You might have felt this as you read about the previous generations in this book. Maybe you read about Henry "Box" Brown and imagined being crammed into that crate. Along with him, your muscles tightened and your breath got a little shallower. Or you might have imagined crossing the bridge at Selma, marching into what looked like hundreds of state troopers, armed and ready for a fight. Maybe your heart beat just a little faster. You might have had this response to Bessie Coleman or Bill Russell or even stories you've read outside of this book.

With each new story, your mind prepared your body for what was to come. Even if you didn't consciously think about what it would feel like to be in their position, your brain saw something coming, and it helped you brace for the impact.

The wisdom and strength of previous generations told your brain what to do. As our ancestors experienced heart-breaking, body-numbing suffering, their brains changed. And, as you know well by now, those changes have stuck with us through the generations.

We activate their strength the same way our brains prepare us to shoot like Kobe.

Except, to harness the full power of our transgenerational resiliency, we have to lean into our grit. We must recognize that the inspiration, power, and wisdom of our ancestors is more than just history. It's the secret to propelling ourselves forward to accomplish our goals.

We do that by using our strongest ancestors—whether or not they're related by blood—to spark our positivity cycle.

But that's not enough.

Remember that we're constantly changing our own DNA, building on what our ancestors did to make ourselves even stronger. The concrete barriers we encounter make us stronger, too. These allow us to translate our struggles into future strength for our children, grandchildren, nieces and nephews, or even neighborhood kids.

That means we have to lean into the positivity cycle. As you read the stories in this book and recounted your family memories, you probably felt that tingle of pride. That tingle is the spark in a wildfire.

But for the fire to burn as hot and wide as it can—for your resiliency to become its most powerful—you must give it wind and dry kindling. We do that by recognizing the positivity cycle.

When we feel that spark of positivity, we nurture it with our confidence. We repeat to ourselves that we are strong, powerful, and resilient, and we allow that self-talk to become confidence.

Then we wear that confidence like a badge of honor. We move through our lives like we can accomplish anything.

Because we can.

Henry "Box" Brown did this. He saw the power of his ancestors and peers, and he knew he could do anything. So he shipped himself to freedom.

The marchers at Selma did that, too. They recognized the strength of their parents and grandparents. When they felt anxious and tired, they pushed on because their ancestors had been through much worse. And they won the right to vote.

And Bessie Coleman saw what her family had been through. She used her optimism to propel her halfway around the world, and when others told her she couldn't do what she wanted, she did it anyway.

It wasn't enough for these historical figures to activate their transgenerational resiliency. They also had to nurture it. They had to consciously believe that they could do big, important things, and then they had to follow through.

With the help of our brain's natural tendency to cycle, we can tap into this kind of positivity. But we have to truly believe—in our bones—that we carry the strength of our ancestors. To do this, we need to know what that strength looks like.

We need to imagine our strongest ancestor.

EXERCISE: YOUR STRONGEST ANCESTOR

You've been thinking about your ancestors throughout this book. By tracing your relationship to them and writing or drawing a story about their optimism, you've prepared yourself to draw from their strength in your own challenges.

In this exercise, we'll extend our progress to target their strength. The exercise will ask you to think of your strongest ancestor, and that person will become the spark that activates your positivity cycle.

Gather Supplies

Begin by gathering a sheet of paper and some drawing supplies. You can just use a pen or pencil or crayons and markers.

Choose Your Strongest Ancestor

Now, choose your strongest ancestor. You should have plenty of choices noted on your genogram, but you may also choose to imagine someone else—possibly even someone from this book. After all, even if the famous African Americans in this book weren't truly related to you, they still contributed to our strength—they're still our ancestors.

List Their Traits

At the top of the page, list five or six of their strongest traits. These might be things like "determination," "intelligence," "way with words," or "patience." Whichever words you choose, remember that they should be positive traits. In this exercise, we aren't focusing on the concrete barriers they faced—we're focusing on the things that helped them overcome those barriers. List those terms and take a moment to reflect on what they mean and why they inspire you.

Draw Your Ancestor

Finally, without thinking too much about it, draw your ancestor. Channel your ancestors' strength, their positive traits, and their resiliency onto the page. The point isn't to create a beautiful drawing. The point is to let your ancestors' strength and resiliency flow through you and into your drawing.

Include your ancestor as well as their environment. Where were they when they were at their strongest? What were they doing? How did they look? Who was with them?

Add enough detail to really give a sense of who they were and how they felt.

Reflection

Finally, on a separate sheet of paper, write a quick paragraph about what you drew. How did you capture their strongest traits? What did you imagine when you thought of them? How did it make you feel? Are you proud of them? Inspired? Amazed? Add those feelings to your paragraph.

Look back over what you wrote and drew, and remember that your ancestors' strength is in your DNA.

ACTIVATING TRANSGENERATIONAL RESILIENCY: KEY POINTS

The previous sections of this book have focused on exploring the psychology of transgenerational resiliency. In this section, we pushed ourselves to activate that resiliency. The most important point of this section is that you *know* you are strong and resilient—you just need to accept it. Let's review the key points that brought us to that realization.

Identity

The first step to activating our transgenerational resiliency is embracing who we are. No matter what society pressures us to be, we are strongest when we know who we are—strong, powerful, resilient African Americans. Embracing that identity allows us to play both defense and offense with the wisdom and epigenetic strength of our ancestors.

Optimism

It's important to see the world for what it truly is, recognizing the concrete barriers it places in front of us. But the only way to break through those barriers is by embracing our ancestors' optimism. When we apply their optimistic thinking to our own life challenges, we become unstoppable. Embracing our optimism helps us achieve our own goals and teach other African Americans around us that they can win, too.

The Positivity Cycle

Just as anxiety can cycle through our minds, positivity can

become a cycle, too. Our knowledge of African American history is like a spark. It encourages us to move forward with optimism and courage. When we feel that spark of positivity, we have to lean into it, using the confidence to build positive outcomes. We can motivate ourselves by learning about our family's history and African American history in general. And with the knowledge we gain, we can keep our positivity cycle moving forward, propelling us to achieve our dreams.

CONCLUSION

There are many ways to make a sword.

But some field swords are created through fire. Japanese sword smiths, in particular, coat their swords in clay. Some areas of the sword are given thicker coats to protect the surface from overheating. Other areas are more thinly packed. When the clay has been layered onto the sword, the weapon is run through fire until it is both sharp and durable.

Heat typically makes metal weaker.

But, in this case, the clay packed on the sword's steel protects the metal. It's a barrier to the firing process, which uses extreme heat followed by extreme cool to create strength. Without that clay, the process can ruin an otherwise beautiful sword.

That clay is like transgenerational resiliency.

Think back to the many challenges our ancestors have faced. From the transatlantic slave trade to Jim Crow to segregation and violence, African Americans have not only survived. We've thrived.

We didn't crumble under that unrelenting pressure.

We channeled that fiery heat into power. By collecting the wisdom of our ancestors, we learned how to stand in the face of efforts to murder us. And through that survival, our brains changed.

Epigenetic strength collected around us like a snowball—like the clay around a sword—building and building until we were protected. Until we could withstand anything.

And through that fire, our ancestors grew stronger. They learned to play both defense and offense. They learned to find pockets of optimism. And eventually, those skills became a way of life.

As a military man, I often think back to the African American soldiers who returned from World War II. They had been promised so much for their service—a college education, unemployment insurance, and housing. When they returned home—those who did—they found that the promises weren't really meant for them. They were meant for their white counterparts.

It would have been so easy to just give up.

But they didn't. They embraced the housing they could find and made those neighborhoods their homes.

Their children grew up to be all the things their parents couldn't—doctors and lawyers and government officials in big, beautiful houses across the country.

Racist laws tried to stop them, but they were no match for transgenerational resiliency.

Those concrete barriers worked like a whetstone, honing the crisp edge of a sword until it was razor sharp.

We're the result of that work. After years of heating and honing, our culture produced you—a strong, powerful, optimistic, resilient African American.

Sometimes, it's hard to see that. We face our own concrete barriers and wonder if we can survive all the things the world throws at us. I saw that in so many of my clients—strong, bold men and women who just needed to believe in themselves. They couldn't see that their ancestors were inside them, propping them up and pushing them forward.

That's why I wrote this book. I saw too many of our children facing the world with the false belief that they were weak. When they went out into the world, they crumbled from anxiety and fear, trapped in the loop of negative feelings. They couldn't see the power they had inside them.

But it's there. Whether we realize it or not, our ancestors' power is inside us.

We just have to activate it.

BACK TO RUBY BRIDGES

I opened this book with a reflection on one brave little girl. When I look at that famous picture of Ruby Bridges, marching boldly into school with her head held high, I see transgenerational resiliency in action.

So many people would have melted into a puddle of fear.

After all, there was a lot to be afraid of.

I don't know whether Ruby Bridges knew that she had her ancestors' power inside her.

But she did.

And as frightened as she was, she persisted through that terrible day, and she was alright. The days after were undoubtedly terrible, too. And she was alright. She's still climbing school steps today. She's not fighting for a desk anymore. Now, she teaches children about her story. And while she certainly suffered, her story isn't about pain.

It's about resiliency.

Ruby Bridges, like all of us, had the power of her ancestors' epigenetics in her blood. Through history's multiplication tables, the generations of her family built and rebuilt her brain until she was unstoppable. She must have seen that, as scared as she was. And as she went on to thrive in the face of adversity, her brain must have restructured just a bit. It must have woken up to the intense possibilities it carried. What carried her through those difficult times? How did she fight through the anxiety loop? She must have realized that, even if she failed, her existence in that school made a difference. At the time, I don't know if she knew how much stronger those experiences would make her. But surely she sees it now. Surely, we all do.

We all face concrete barriers like that little girl. Sometimes they're obvious, like white mothers screaming at us as we walk toward the door of a school. Other times, they're more covert, like the hidden racial bias of hiring managers. Every single day we face some barrier or another, large or small, obvious or hidden, deadly or simply inconvenient. Like that little girl, we have a hidden tool that others don't—we've trained all our lives to be one step ahead of those barriers. We can move forward while checking our defenses. When concrete barriers jump out in front of us, we're ready for them. African Americans have seen it all. And we know how to stay standing, moving forward like the powerful black queen.

That power isn't just in our blood. It's in our experiences, too. Too often, we forget that we've been given the gift of our parents, grandparents, aunties, uncles, and community members. We forget what a gift African American history can be.

Until we rediscover the power of those stories.

It starts as a tingle in our chests, those tales of survival, of laughing in the face of extreme persecution. But it grows until our brains are activated with the resiliency of hundreds of years of African American survival.

Armed with their strength, we can stare down anything. We can come through the most difficult things and do much more than survive—we can thrive.

MARCH FORWARD

As you finish this book and put it aside, I hope you'll continue to reflect on the lessons of your ancestors. The exercises you've completed should have taught you the remarkable, unusual strength in your DNA. But recognizing these things is just the first step. Once we've put together the pieces of our empowering heritage, we have to practice using our resiliency. It's not always easy. If you've struggled with the anxiety loop, if you've gotten used to self-defeating actions, or if you've always seen yourself as weak, you may have some work ahead.

But you'll never unsee the connections you've made. It's simply impossible to shut down your resiliency once you've made the connections to your ancestors' strength.

I've seen it over and over again. Sometimes it's an experience. Sometimes it's an emotion. Sometimes it's a story. And sometimes it's a psychological realization.

I can always tell when it's happened, because something clicks. That client stops and says, "wait a minute. I'm stronger than most people around me. I have control of my life. I'm unbreakable."

They're right—they are. And so are you.

NOTES

2. HISTORY'S MULTIPLICATION TABLES

1. American Psychiatric Association. 2013. *Desk Reference to the Diagnostic Criteria from DSM-5* (R). Arlington, TX: American Psychiatric Association Publishing, p. 301-302.

12. KNOW WHO YOU ARE

1. Adapted from George Ella Lyon, *Where I'm From: Where Poems Come From* (Absey & Co, 1999).

Made in the USA
Middletown, DE
20 March 2024

51818174R00115